AN INTRODUCTION TO
Storytelling

AN INTRODUCTION TO

Storytelling

CHRISTINE WILLISON

ON BEHALF OF THE
SOCIETY FOR STORYTELLING

The
History
Press

First published 2018

The History Press
The Mill, Brimscombe Port
Stroud, Gloucestershire, GL5 2QG
www.thehistorypress.co.uk

British Library Cataloguing in Publication Data.
A catalogue record for this book is available from the British Library.

ISBN 978 0 7509 8755 4

Typesetting and origination by The History Press
Printed in Great Britain

Contents

AN INTRODUCTION TO
Storytelling

This is a collection of anecdotes, experiences, explanations and suggestions from storytellers around the world, covering many topics, styles and approaches. From these varied journeys into storytelling, you will see that there are as many avenues into the art form as there are stories within it. So, this is not a 'how to' book, but more of a 'ways of doing it' book. We include storytelling in health, in schools, with people in special needs education, with young children, and in support of language learning. We give hints and tips on style and content. We explore where storytelling sits between truth and lies. Here you will find both practical advice and philosophical insight. Most importantly, we want to engender the love of stories and the fun that can be had. All contributors have agreed to donate any royalties to the Society for Storytelling (www.sfs.org.uk). We thank them all.

Christine Willison
Pembrokeshire, 2018

To Begin

What do we mean by storytelling? It's a term used by writers, film-makers, journalists, actors, puppeteers, poets, readers and others who use story in their art.

All of these are valid, but the Cinderella of the art form is the traditional oral storyteller. No script, no props, no cameras, no books, no pen or paper are required. Just a comfy place to sit and a glass of water and the magic of 'Once Upon a Time…'

Starters

My advice on beginning is to start safe, with your own family or friends, maybe a class in your local school. Children can be your best starting point. You can tell small people the same story every day for several weeks. They love it, feel secure in the familiarity of a known story. You will have time to get to know the story inside out and upside down. It's amazing how much you can discover from a story told repetitively.

Why?

Why do you want to be a storyteller? You may want to tell stories to your family, to recreate a family story, a piece of local history, retell a myth or legend, or revive a childhood story. You may have an occasion like a wedding, funeral, naming ceremony or anniversary coming up at which you would like to tell a story. For some people it's therapy or a form of catharsis. For others it's a way of combatting loneliness, old age or shyness. You may simply want to share something you've heard with an audience or group of friends. There is no right or wrong, but there must be enthusiasm and passion.

Telling Professionally

When you embark on your career as a storyteller, or even if you need to brush up your skills mid-career, most professionals would advise you to look at going on a course. There are some good centres which can provide useful tuition. It is also good to engage with others since storytelling can be quite a lonely occupation. In addition, you could join the Society for Storytelling, who have edited this book, or Cybermouth, the Bleddfa Centre in Wales, Halsway Manor and other relevant societies/places. Many parts of the UK and around the world have storytelling clubs, where you can meet in a friendly non-threatening environment and try out your new skills or air a new story.

Arm yourself with a library of books (see my suggested reading at the end of this chapter). Be prepared to translate these texts into the totally different form of oral storytelling. This can take a long time. I have stories in my own repertoire that I have been telling since the 1980s, but I still find new ways, voices, additions and refinements each time I tell them.

Be shameless. When you hear a good story, well told, use it. Not verbatim, obviously, but take away the bare bones and add yourself into the story by working and working at it. The only exceptions I would mention are stories you may hear from native Americans and Aboriginal Australians. I remember Uncle Larry Walsh telling a story in Footscray Arts Centre in Victoria, when a member of the audience asked if she could use the story. His robust retort was, 'We have had our land stolen, our children stolen, please don't steal our stories.' So please respect sensitivities, and ask. I remember too someone phoning to congratulate me on the publication of my book *Pembrokeshire Folk Tales* (The History Press) and asking if she could use some of them as told stories. I explained that these were stories which belong to all of us, so please feel free, but please credit your source, which was readily agreed.

Most storytellers will refine and adapt a story over years until they have a performance/sharing of which they are proud and can truly call their own. But don't let that put you off. The refining process can happen through performance and through workshops and sessions in schools.

Do not fall into the trap of scripting and retelling. Whilst you may be pleased with the result, it can also ensnare you. The joy of the oral tradition is the two-way process. The eye contact with your audience. You know if they are with you by the look in their eyes or, alternatively, if they are not with you because they are fidgeting, making trips to the loo or looking out of the window. A good storyteller will adapt their language to ensure the engagement of their audience; this is not possible if the performance is conforming to a script.

In theatres, storytellers like to tell with the house lights up so that they can engage with their audiences.

How Did We Get Here?

I will firstly tell my own story about how I got started, then other storytellers and members of the Society for Storytelling will describe their journey into this land of myth and legend. In addition, storytellers from all over the world have contributed a piece about their own brand of storytelling.

Christine's Journey

We all come to storytelling via a different road. Mine began at the age of five. I started school in 1950. It was a difficult time for schools. Most teachers had just returned from active service in the Second World War. There was a certain amount of retraining required. As a result, our teachers were a mixture of unqualified people or elderly teachers brought out of retirement. We knew that the old woman who taught us in the mornings would, if we kept very quiet, fall asleep. So, we crept around and talked in whispers until we heard snoring coming from her chair in the corner of the room. Then we knew we were safe to tell stories. My stories were mostly about fairies and magic, whilst Ronnie McQuinn's all seemed to involve wild animals. We had to keep him until last because eventually the roaring of lions and tigers woke up our teacher. I wonder what happened to Ronnie?

Whilst these stories were childlike and not memorable, I learnt some useful techniques about the uses of voice and silence and reading your audience, which I still employ.

I took up the art again when I became a mother, with three small children under the age of five.

When my own children were all at school, I volunteered as a classroom helper, listening to children reading, sharing some of my skills as an artist. I discovered that one of the main barriers to reading was unfamiliarity with books. Many children didn't see their parents read, didn't join the library and didn't have any reading material at home. Where I lived in rural East Anglia, there were marvellous bookshops in Norwich and Ipswich, but these were not really accessible to many young people. I decided to create a travelling bookshop. I managed to persuade the literature officer of my local arts association to facilitate a grant. The climate for arts funding such a project was healthy. I got a youth employment project interested in doing some practical work, and we converted a caravan. I bought a towing vehicle, opened accounts with book publishers and wholesalers, and booked appointments in schools in the (then) six counties of East Anglia. I also raised funds from the Arts Council of Great Britain (as it was then) and the Gulbenkian Foundation. Everyone could see the value of this not-for-profit 'community' bookshop (profits on books were applied to the running costs).

For seven years I drove my Ford Cortina towing a Sprite Caravan, suitably painted with reproductions of Brian Froud's wonderful goblins (thanks again Brian for permission) into the school playgrounds of East Anglia. I went into each classroom and in these sessions with children I helped them to understand the business of writing, publishing, selling and buying books.

We looked at the book as an object, at the elements of the book, at the précis on the back as an aid to making a choice, at the ISBN which helps to trace a book in libraries and bookshops, and at information about pricing, and why prices in the US, South Africa and Australia are sometimes included.

We talked about the writers of books, about the writing process, submission to publishers, the rejection slips which usually outnumber acceptance letters.

I introduced them to new authors and new books by their favourite writers; supporting even the most reticent reader with advice, suggestions, readings and storytelling; encouraging the sharing of oral stories with people who shied away from the written word.

Then each class had time to browse and buy. Parents came after school to share the experience and do their own browsing and buying. It was very successful.

A favourite piece of feedback was the girl who, unable to buy anything through lack of money on my first visit to her school, got a paper round and saved all her wages to spend when I repeated my visit to her school.

Arts funding then started to feel the pinch, with less money available, and certainly no funds for capital projects such as replacing the, by now, ailing caravan and tow vehicle. So I changed direction. I still visited schools, still did book sessions, including readings and storytelling, but now I set up small bookshops in each of the schools I visited.

Other publishers/organisations emulated Bookbug. Some headteachers were seduced by 'profits', by donations of free books and cash to the school library. Time for another change.

I now devoted myself to full-time storytelling. What joy to visit schools, arts centres, museums and festivals, requiring only a chair and a glass of water (no caravan load of books) – together with, most importantly, a head full of stories.

Storytelling is an ancient art. Before music (although of course storytelling has a music all of its own), before the sharing of images, before dance, there were stories. All you need is a teller and a listener. Preferably a fire, a comfy seat and fellow listeners, but most of all a teller who knows you, has a notion of your experiences, your grasp of language and imagery, and has a good story to tell. You will notice that a good storyteller shares a story differently with each audience depending on the look in your eyes and the inspiration which emanates from you.

An example from my repertoire is 'The Singing Ringing Tree', which I have been telling for over thirty years. I relish the tale for its anarchy, the tantrums of that dreadful princess, modelled on those of my oldest daughter (the one with the red hair!), its imagery, which I set in our ancient woodland here in Wales, and the transformation of the princess through survival tactics. I discover something new about this tale every time I tell it. Recently my partner and I have created a version of this tale with piano accompaniment. It's quite a challenge for a pianist to gather prompts for music from the impromptu style of the oral tradition.

Themes and Elements

Before I hand on the baton to the other storytellers, I will mention themes. They help the memory cells to order a story.

Firstly, of course, I don't need to tell you that a good story should have a beginning, a middle and an end. Sometimes these are the most difficult things to refine (especially the end, in my experience). You need a character. There is usually a mission, journey or problem to solve. Then no matter how much you try to avoid it, you will include the four elements of Earth, Wind (Air), Fire and Water.

Earth can be a forest, a mountain, five magic beans, a house of straw, one of sticks and another of bricks – all from the earth.

Wind often blows wisdom, messages, a storm on land or at sea. Wind can be the flight of a bird, dragon, person, broomstick. The huffing and puffing of a wolf come to blow the house down.

Fire is where we gather to tell stories, where we cook, it is our sentinel whilst sheltering in the woodland. It can be the sparks that fly from an angry sorcerer's nose, the fire in the hearth at the bottom of the chimney in a brother pig's brick house.

Water Our journey may take us over the sea, across the river, maidens may appear from a lake or pond. Water may magically become ice. The Spirit of the Well can help to protect a house against the intrusion of twelve witches. Water is in the pot, on the fire at the bottom of the chimney which scalds the wolf to death when he climbs down the chimney.

So, our hero may take a journey through the forest, she may meet a creature who can help her on her journey by giving, perhaps an artefact or token which enables the power of flight. When she shelters in the forest she builds a fire to keep warm and to protect from wild animals. She then has to ask a ferryman to take her across the river… and so on.

Artefacts

The following is my list of items useful in stories. I hope it will assist you to make your own list.

Key

The key could fit a door or a box. Perhaps the key fits into the lock on a box? Has the box been found in the attic, covered with dust? The box is opened to reveal… nothing or something? Maybe a map, a sword, a jewel, a book of spells, or a pair of boots.

Door or Portal

Here in Wales you need help in the search for a way through to the Otherworld. In some tales a door magically opens in the side of a mountain or in the trunk of a tree. Maybe there are three doors, the key fits only one of them and you can escape, but if you try the key in either of the other doors it'll be the worse for you!

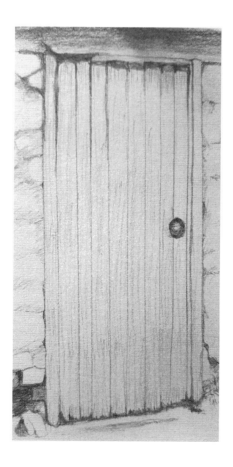

Box

A box is a lovely thing in a story. It may be huge – big enough to get inside, but beware if you close the lid. It may be tiny, with a magic spell inside, a magic stone, a lucky charm. Maybe the very act of opening the box sparks off some magic. It may be big enough to contain any or all of the other items on this list.

Map

Perhaps the map was inside the box? Does it show the place where treasure is buried? Does it tell where a princess is held captive? Will it help you to find the entrance to the Otherworld?

Stone

Stone soup, the sword in the stone, a stone to be rolled aside to reveal a portal or staircase going down into the darkness. A standing stone behind which to hide whilst you observe the fairies in their dance.

Sword

To guard our hero, point the way, used by a King to bestow favours, to kill the snake hiding under the rug in the bride's room. To kill the poisonous toad blocking the flow of water into the well of life-giving water.

Pot, Crock or Jug

Ceridwen's cauldron, the pot at the bottom of the lake hiding the princess from her rescuer, the Magic Porridge Pot, the crock of gold that every self-respecting Leprechaun has hidden somewhere.

Basket

For taking produce to market, goodies to Grandma's house in the forest, for collecting artefacts to enable you to journey through the place of stories.

Apple

Here my dear, take an apple from my basket... the rejuvenating apples that give eternal life, the apple thrown to a wounded warrior by his guardian spirit – he takes a bite from the apple and it becomes whole again and sustains him until he is rescued.

Ring

Thanks to **J.R.R.** Tolkien for using this token to good effect. There is the ring that makes the wearer invisible, the inscription which takes you on the journey, the ring that can't be removed once placed on your finger.

Trees and Forests

The Singing Ringing Tree, the forest where small girls encounter wolves, the home of the charcoal burner, the place where you visit Grandma, there will be a woodsman with the axe, a place to lose a couple of children. In days gone by, most of Europe was covered in forest, so every day your journey inevitably included time spent in the woodland.

Shoe or Boot

Cinderella's glass slipper, Puss in Boots, slippers by the fire, the shoemaker who receives help in the night from two elves…

Loaf of Bread

The Little Red Hen after getting no help to gather grain, make flour or make bread, eats the bread herself. The miller's sons grinding grain and heaving sacks of flour, stop work to listen to a bird singing on the roof. The mill wheel brings about the demise of the murdering woman. The loaf which, when cut, reveals more than just crumbs.

Nail

For the want of a nail the shoe was lost…, a coffin nail, a clue about horse and rider, a place to hang your coat, the bent nails and pins placed around a sacred well to ward off evil spirits.

Candlestick

The candle flame flickered… Little Nancy Etticoat in a white petticoat, the longer she stands the shorter she grows. With a candlestick in the library…

Cup or Goblet

A goblet, chalice or cup appears and reappears in stories. She held the cup to his lips... He dropped the potion into a goblet of wine... A fly fell off the overhead beam, landed in milady's goblet. Unnoticed, she drank the contents, nine months later she bore a child...

Jewel

The search for the precious diamond. The gem which was lost from the Queen's necklace, a precious stone set in the lid of a box.

Book

A book of spells, a book found in the attic. An inscription on the flyleaf, a note left in Chapter 13. There are many ways of using the book as a device in stories.

Finally, and most importantly – Cloth

You will know I'm sure about the relationship of stories to textiles, not just the maiden challenged to turn flax into gold, but the whole genre is interwoven with cloth, weaving, spinning, cutting, sewing.

A story is woven like cloth, it's knitted together, a yarn is spun, its thread or line can transport and empower its audience. We embroider text with metaphor, with colour, with drama. Textiles form the warp and weft of our thoughts. The wide boy will have the whole thing sewn up. Text began as a loom of interwoven threads. Textiles provide us with *tweedy, woollen, home-spun, russet*, describing rustic, rude or ignorant characters. In this book we have a *patchwork of stories and story-related experiences.*

Suggested Reading

Arnott, Kathleen *African Myths and Legends*, Oxford University Press, 2000

Briggs, Katherine *A Dictionary of Fairy Tales*, Penguin, 1993

Calvino, Italo *Italian Folk Tales*, Penguin, 2000

Carter, Angela *The Second Virago Book of Fairy Tales*, Virago, 1992

Davies, Sioned (trans.) *The Mabinogion*, Oxford University Press, 2008

Dean Guie, Heister (ed.) *Coyote Stories*, University of Nebraska Press, 1990

Opie, Iona and Peter *Classic Fairy Tales*, Paladin Press, 1980

Shedlock, Marie L., *The Art of The Story-Teller*, Dover, 2003

Squire, Charles *Mythology of the Celtic People*, Bracken Books, 1996

Warner, Marina *Once Upon a Time, a Short History of Fairy Tale*, Oxford University Press, 2014

There are loads more – please visit my website or email me on: christinestories@yahoo.co.uk

Finding Your Own Route

JOHN ROW

This storytelling business is, for me, the most exciting, rewarding and satisfying aspect of a life spent scraping a living from the arts. At the same time, it is full of frustrations.

Once bitten by the storytelling bug I became a prospector. When I was first asked to tell stories, I searched through the mountain of books in my own home to find collections of folk tales accidentally acquired from subscribing to obscure book clubs that had long since ceased to exist. As my enthusiasm grew I scoured second-hand bookshops for those prized volumes written at the turn of the twentieth century as industrialisation moved populations from the land to the city, empires collapsed and rose, and national consciousness grew in country after country and writers scurried here and there writing down scraps of stories from old men and women. I even became a collector myself, sitting in bars on the northern fringe of Europe in the early hours listening to beautiful young tourist guides who told me stories their grandmothers had told them and men who had ambitions to drive husky teams across the old reindeer routes from Lapland to Alaska.

I took every opportunity I could get to listen and get to know the giants, Hugh Lupton, Duncan Williamson and a host of others. Each teller made me realise how far I had to go on my own journey. I felt and still feel a rank amateur in comparison.

However, with the conceit of the beginner and with the need to earn a living from one artistic activity or another, I called myself a storyteller, even duplicating a leaflet calling myself 'John Row, The Story Man', which I had the audacity to hand out in the bar of the Queen Elizabeth Hall at a storytelling festival that included Hugh, Duncan, Ben Haggarty and Louise Bennet. The thought makes me cringe now, but it is not something I regret. Self-belief, even if it is at times delusional, is a powerful engine and helps keep up the momentum as we journey on even further on our chosen path.

It helped that I was broke, having lost my position as bookshop manager at Colchester Arts Centre when the Eastern Arts Association decided to stop subsidising the shop. I had been given the post as a way for the then Literature Officer of the Association, Laurence Staig, to keep me alive as a poet. During my time there I had seen the Company of Storytellers, who rekindled an interest in storytelling in me. Before seeing them, it had never occurred to me that this was a way to make a living, but their inspiration was an important step in my journey. The final push came from the wonderful Tarby Davenport, the unsung heroine of the East Anglian arts scene who has probably done more than anyone I know to bring quality unusual performance into the public arena. Calling in at her

cottage on the way back from a poetry reading, she mentioned it was a pity I wasn't a storyteller because she could give me some work. 'By an amazing coincidence, I am!' I replied and so began my voyage into unchartered waters.

In retrospect I had been unconsciously preparing for this my whole life. I grew up without television and listening to *Children's Hour* every evening on the wireless there was always a story. Before I went to bed my mother would always read me a folk tale or a poem from our set of Arthur Mee's Encyclopaedias. I still remember the excitement of visiting The Ideal Home Exhibition at Earls Court where the salesman convinced my parents to buy this treasure trove of fact and fiction. This was how we spent our evenings as we waited for my dad to come home on leave from whichever ship or air station he was serving on at the time. Once home I would listen wide-eyed to stories of his travels, poring through old photo albums of his pre-war navy life; I was fascinated by his accounts of crossing the line (the equator) and King Neptune. He talked for hours of his early days at sea and of the hardships and adventures of his youth on Vancouver Island (a journey he made alone by boat and train from Sudbury in Suffolk at the age of fifteen).

These were my foundations which I continued to accidentally build on later in life when, after many of my own adventures, I decided to write about a time traveller. Dressing as a medieval pedlar I walked around Essex, Suffolk and Norfolk, living as Samuel Partridge, pedlar of Beccles. To add substance to my character I learned a few East Anglian tales, telling them along the way. I never did write the book, but the experience was invaluable when, eight years later, I decided to ply my trade as a storyteller.

I was lucky in at least one respect in that I did not have a problem standing up and performing in front of people. I had spent over twenty years as a performance poet taking poetry into areas not used to hearing it. Touring with Nick Toczek in Stereo Graffiti we took over hotel dining rooms in Edinburgh during the Fringe, where we picked up a local audience, and were studiously ignored by the regulars in Yorkshire working men's clubs.

In Ipswich Arts Theatre where my wife, Rose, worked as theatre electrician we put on free Monday night shows, combining poetry with the theatre of the absurd. There, Pam Ferris taught me that the stage was not a great desert but a space that could be covered in a few paces. All this was training for my future as a storyteller; a little random, maybe, but all useful.

Having got a head full of stories, or at least enough to cover an hour or so of performance, I soon realised that even if I could get the work I was nowhere near ready. I tried to sound like the storytellers I had heard, people who leant forward as if imparting great secrets to their audiences. Their stories gradually unfolded, sucking the listener in, creating spaces in the mind where anything could and generally did happen.

I tried, but I felt I was wearing handcuffs. I was from a world of rock 'n' roll, jazz and performance poetry, an Essex boy, born in Barking and growing up in Harlow New Town. I did not have, as was pointed out to me later in my career, a storyteller's accent. Gradually it dawned on me that things might improve if I stopped pretending to be someone I wasn't.

I recalled the words of the great jazz trumpeter, Miles Davis: 'Sometimes it takes a long time to play like yourself.'

I remember storytelling to a group of foreign students at the University of East Anglia. At the end a Japanese man came up to me and asked in a mild-mannered voice, 'Please, how do I become a storyteller?' All I could say was the first thing he had to do was to forget everything he had seen me do. It was obvious that my somewhat flamboyant style would have been a disaster for him to try and emulate.

I have always dressed up to perform. I think it give me a freedom to be expansive. It is like dressing to go out for the evening or to go to a job interview. It was and still is my public self. One half of who I am. When I started telling, I took Samuel Partridge back out of the wardrobe and became my medieval self. But this was too time-specific for me, so I reverted to the top hat I had retrieved from a dustbin in Birmingham fifteen years earlier when I was with Stereo Graffiti. There was an old dame school being emptied next to our drummer's house and I watched all kinds of treasures go into the bin, dance cards from 1920s cruises, tins of coronation chocolate, Aston Villa season tickets from the 1890s and an immaculate silk topper. This became the basis of a look that has stood me in good stead for a quarter of a century.

There are those that say a costume gets in the way of the story. This may be true for some people, but we dress for each occasion in the way that makes us most comfortable and relaxed, and storytelling is no different. Apart from that I tell a lot of open-air events, offering stories to individual families. If I was dressed in jeans and a T-shirt they might understandably call the nearest constable. The costume seems to legitimise me.

Storytelling in the open-air was something I drifted into, partly by choice, partly by necessity, but mainly through coincidence.

Margaret Thatcher's attack on the public sector meant the arts would inevitably come in the firing line and soon for all but the best-known names, subsidies began to disappear. As well as losing my position at Colchester Arts Centre and the closure of the bookshop, the regional Writers in Schools scheme was decimated. No longer were local artists supported in any way financially, but even my income from touring schools as a visiting poet vanished.

There were many advantages to cutting my teeth on the do-it-yourself culture of Ipswich and London in the 1960s, the Albion Fairs in the 1970s and the punk explosion in the 1980s, one of which was to realise it is possible to create your own audiences and circuits without relying on any establishment to do it for you.

I went back to my own people, that mixture of beats, hippies, anarchists and greens, and individuals like Tarby, who had been immersed in the folk culture since the early 1960s and who started promoting because she couldn't find anything she wanted to see in her own area.

She booked me for events around Suffolk put on by councils who had not yet felt the full effects of austerity. Strawberry Fair in Cambridge opened up the festival circuit for me through one of those coincidental conversations. I was taking a break between telling at the fair and chatting with Tony

Cordy when I mentioned that it was disgusting that an old hippy like me had never been to Glastonbury. He was running Green Kidz that year and gave me two tickets and some diesel money to come and tell stories. That was in 1991 and I have been working for Tony – who has been running Glastonbury Festival's Kidz Field for over twenty years – ever since.

But sitting and waiting for the phone to ring when few people know you exist does not bring home either the bacon or the tofu, so I devised a plan to get some regional publicity.

I went to Charlie Mannings, who had the fairground at Felixstowe. It was the beginning of the season and we both needed publicity. I asked if I could busk at the fairground in front of one of the rides for the season so we could get some coverage in the local and regional newspapers. The plan worked, and we got a good spread in both the *Ipswich Evening Star* and the *East Anglian Daily Times*, one of the biggest regional newspapers in the country.

I hardly made any money, but it taught me a lot about working an open-air audience and for years afterwards I would meet children in schools all over the country who remembered seeing me at the fair.

For the next couple of years I would tell stories anywhere people would have me. Some festivals got me for the price of a ticket, but only once. The next year they paid. My reputation as an open-air teller grew and Cambridge City Council booked me for their 'Summer in the City' programme and from this came the Folk Festival where, with the support of the then director Eddie Barcan, I established the storytelling area.

Forever trying to get storytelling into areas where it was not established, I told in holiday destinations from Center Parcs (where Christine Willison, the editor of this collection, was already telling) to Lapland. I became the first Storyteller in Residence in a British prison, and got the first publicity for the now well-established Storybook Dads scheme, and have visited schools on four continents.

It has been wonderful and frustrating. There have been times when it was difficult to get work in schools because I was thought of as just an

open-air performer and keeping an eye on the ever-changing goal posts in the arts world gets more difficult as the years progress, but I chose my own path, so I have no complaints.

I still swing between feeling like a charlatan and a complete novice as I watch a fantastic array of new tellers come on the scene cutting their own swathe.

Meanwhile I rejoice at the opportunities I have had and am still having as I sit on a mountain in Romania collecting yet more stories.

Stepping Stones

KEVIN CROSSLEY-HOLLAND

Most young children hear stories, and follow them on screens, well before they can fully understand them or read them for themselves.

John Stuart Mill was right when he wrote of childhood memory as 'the present consciousness of a past sensation'; and applied to the first hearing of a story, that consciousness is primarily of the music of story – that's to say the music of language – which is all the more significant in this modern generation besotted by the visual.

Think of the pulsing beat, repetition and rhyme within nursery rhymes that we carry with us all our lives, and love to introduce to our own children and grandchildren. 'This little piggy went to market' is unforgettable. 'There was once a very small pig who went to the market' is not.

I don't have anything like total recall of my childhood – who does? – but when I was six or seven my mother taught me simple memory techniques. I used them then, and I still do. But earlier still...

My sister is lying on the bottom of our bunk bed; I am on the top. My father is sitting beside us, cradling his Welsh harp and singing-and-saying a story. Sometimes pausing (because silence is part of performance) and smiling an ineffable smile. I was utterly mesmerised. My father was away during the weekdays in far London, and I could scarcely wait for the weekends, walking with him in the beechwoods, dragging home branches to be sawn up for the fire, combing Iron Age sites for potsherds, setting up my shed-museum, and in the evenings listening to Welsh and Irish and Scottish and Manx and Cornish tales. They mattered so much to me. And so did the fact that it was my father who was telling them, though I couldn't have explained why.

My memories of all this – not only the music and meaning of the stories but the sights and sounds and smells in our little nursery in the Chilterns – are, after seventy years, so sharp-edged. They don't go away; they come close, and become more vivid.

G.K. Chesterton wrote of his memory of childhood being 'a sort of white light on everything, cutting things out very clearly, and [rather] emphasising their solidity. The point is that the white light had a sort of wonder in it, as if the world were as new as myself...' That's is how I too see many scenes from my childhood, and above all my father storytelling to us.

And yet, what exactly is it that mattered to me so much? And what matters now? And how can it contribute to making sense of my life?

Well, to begin with, a parent is sharing with his or her children, and they relish that. They adore it. And what the parent is sharing is nuggets of experience in the shape of stories, arresting in themselves, and akin to stepping-stones a child crosses to greater self-awareness. Stepping-stones informed by the full gamut of human experience, serious and playful, that slowly help to lead children into what Robert Coles called the 'moral imagination': an understanding of the love, friendship, and empathy we humans can offer, and what we mistrust, dislike, fear… how, in short, we may live more decent, neighbourly lives.

Is there actually anything more important than this?

When God pities Adam and Eve after throwing them out of Eden, he tells them he still loves them and gives them a pearl. This pearl, he says, is a tear. God tells Adam and Eve that they'll see terrible suffering in the world, and weep tears, but that their tears will lighten their sorrow a little.

This exquisite Jewish traditional tale makes plain that individual experience within any folk tale is also representative of an idea, an intention, a feeling, an action, a consequence we have all experienced.

Not that folk tales show that we are all alike. Deriving from different cultures and belief systems, they often demonstrate that we are unalike – and of course the implication is that we should accept people for who they are, not whom we want them to be.

Set beside all this, I realise anew that while there are plainly differences between storytellers and retellers (such as I am), and that those differences are well worth discussing, they matter much less than the crucial act of storytelling itself.

As I argued long since in a paper published in the Society for Storytelling Oracle series ('*Different* – but oh how like'), we should all spend time inhabiting the world of traditional tale and not retell or rewrite without having some knowledge of the culture from which our chosen tale comes; we must get to grips with a tale's core – what it meant to its first audience and, crucially, how we may want to recast it; we must find a voice neither fatty or complicated but simple and lean, bearing in mind that traditional tale deals in action always, seldom in feelings or ideas; and whether as storytellers or writers, we must take account of our audience, their innocence, their experience.

For the most part, our responsibilities are shared ones and, from my own experience as a student of oral tradition and reteller of traditional tale, drafting, paring down, listening, redrafting, has only increased my delight in hearing a fine storyteller at work and play.

You and I, and everyone who tells, retells or draws on the coloured hoard of traditional tales – we are, as Ralph Vaughan Williams described his settings of folk-songs, 'new leaves on an old tree'. Saying-and-singing. Always the same; never the same.

Taking Charge of our Lives through Storytelling: A Memoir

JACK ZIPES

I was never meant to be a storyteller – that is, a conscious and critical storyteller, careful to use words for their most potent effect. Yet, somehow, I have become one, and I am not alone or unusual. Every living human being is capable of becoming a conscious and critical storyteller. But most never reach this goal, and the reason is clear. We, and especially our children, are bombarded with hundreds of diverting and deceptive messages through the mass media, religious and political institutions, schools and colleges, and powerful corporations every day so that our minds become blurred, and we can barely think for ourselves or articulate our needs and desires. While the bombardment of our lives through commercial and political storytelling fosters muddy thinking and conformism to messages that sustain the current socio-economic systems, it is also storytelling that can paradoxically liberate us to a great degree from constraints that inhibit us from realizing deeply felt wishes and drives.

As a child growing up in a nouveau riche Jewish family in Mount Vernon, New York, all I knew and felt was that I was supposed to become a success no matter what profession I intended to pursue. Secretly, I always wanted to be a writer, the next great American writer, and that is why I chose to study for a PhD in American Literature at Columbia University, against my father's wishes. He had expected more 'practicality' from me and refused to support me after I made my choice to live the life of a 'poor man' in ivory towers, as he said. I admit that I decided to become a professor not because I wanted to teach but because I needed to earn some kind of a living that would allow me to write the great American novel and free myself from my family. I seemed to have had a plan and seemed to know what I was doing.

In the fall of 1967, after teaching in Germany for two years and accepting a position as Assistant Professor in the German Department at New York University (NYU), my plan collapsed. Different messages from the civil rights groups, the anti-Vietnam War and the Women's Movement swamped my mind and challenged everything that I believed about myself, American democracy and freedom of choice. I remember reading the great Herbert Marcuse's provocative book, *The One-Dimensional Man*, and realising that I was just that, a one-dimensional man. However, like thousands of other young people at that time, I rebelled against one-dimensional thinking and sought to speak truth to power in my teaching. Gone were my thoughts to become the next great American novelist. In the spring of 1970, when five students at Kent State University were killed in protests against the Vietnam War, I was chosen by the NYU strike committee to join other universities and lead a strike at NYU to stop the killing and the war. I accepted, knowing it would end my career at NYU. In fact, not only did this occur, but I was also blacklisted by most American universities.

In 1972, I was fortunate to find a job in the German Department of the University of Wisconsin-Milwaukee, and that is where I became aware of professional storytelling and storytelling in general. My research began to be focused on folklore and fairy tales and the impact these stories had on children and their socialization. In addition, I became involved with a children's theater in Berlin called Grips, which created and performed radical political plays for children. By 1974, I had translated several Grips plays and tried to have them produced in America without success. Encouraged by a good friend at that time, Ronnie Davis of the San Francisco Mime Troup, I formed my own children's theater called C-Sense. The actors were mainly students, and together we performed the Grips plays for two years until I burned out. Teaching at the university and working every day with the actors exhausted me, but I learned a valuable lesson.

One time in 1976, when I went to an elementary school to determine what the students of a class had liked about a play they had seen, I asked several groups of children to re-enact scenes from the play, and I was amazed by their recall and ingenuity in 'recreating' the scenes. Then they wrote summaries of the plays and illustrated their stories. By the end of two hours, they had touched something magical in my mind: I realized I wanted to become a storyteller, not just for children but also for myself. I had a lot to learn.

During the next few years, I read numerous books about the art of storytelling, the reception of stories by children, child psychology and socialization, game theory, and improvisational theater. I also began teaching a course on storytelling in the University of Wisconsin's Summer College for Kids. Finally, after I read Bruno Bettelheim's *The Uses of Enchantment: The Meaning and Importance of Fairy Tales* in 1976, I became so infuriated by his pedantic and absurd interpretations of how children need and respond to fairy tales that I decided it was time to do my own empirical research; in part to prove how wrong and destructive he was and in part to discover more about how children reacted to fairy tales. Consequently, by 1980, I spent a year at an elementary school in Milwaukee, working with a third-grade teacher once a week for two hours to test my program of storytelling, designed to assist children to become storytellers of their own lives. The focus was to be on the children as storytellers. My stories were to animate them to create and think out of the box.

During the next fifteen years, I continued to develop my ideas and practice of storytelling and came under the influence of Gianni Rodari (1920–1980), the most innovative writer for children in Italy, and I translated his book *The Grammar of Fantasy*. This book became my 'bible', so to speak, and I freely adapted and honed Rodari's ideas so that they would be useful in different ways in my program. Wherever I went – England, Ireland, Germany, Slovenia, many US cities – I tried to demonstrate how my storytelling program would enable children to develop their talents as storytellers, writers, actors, and artists. By 1990 I had moved to Minneapolis to teach at the University of Minnesota. There, through a series of fortuitous events and encounters, I was able in 1995 to obtain a large grant from the Open Foundation in New York City, to collaborate with The Children's Theatre Company of Minneapolis to found a program called Neighborhood Bridges. For the first time in my work as storyteller, I was able to train actors – that is, teaching artists to introduce my program into the public schools of Minneapolis and St Paul. The purpose of the program was to build bridges in schools and communities through storytelling, to grasp how children can learn from each other, to cooperate, and foster greater understanding between different groups of people. Late in life I was learning what it meant to become a conscious and critical storyteller; not by performing to celebrate myself and my talents, but to animate young children to develop confidence in themselves so that they could tell their own stories to articulate their needs, wishes, and plans to live a life of their own choosing.

It may seem somewhat paradoxical to claim that the most meaningful storytelling I have done, and still do, is through abdicating the central role of storyteller and by passing this role on to children (and adults). Yet I have found that telling tales that provoke, animate, assist, or move children to want to tell their own stories and replace mine, or to contend with the

general messages that they hear, has enabled me to understand those differences among us that spring from the ground like a hundred flowers that need to bloom and flourish together through careful cultivation. Moreover, I have had the good fortune to have encountered numerous professional and amateur storytellers in the US and in the UK, who have taught me how to improve my program and my particular style and purpose of storytelling.

Philosophically speaking, which means honestly speaking, I am not convinced that we can ever take complete charge of our lives. On the other hand, I am convinced that life is worthless unless we endeavour to assume complete control of our lives. I also believe that it is crucial to any democratic society that children are encouraged to learn to express their thoughts and desires openly, through stories and anecdotes that project possibilities for them to fulfil their dreams.

Over 200 years ago, William Wordsworth claimed that the child is the father of man. Of course, today we would say that the child is the mother and father of women and men. It is through children and their stories that we learn our failings and qualities, that we learn to take some charge of our lives, even though we are powerless to ward off the intrusions of monsters and dragons. Through story, we learn that we have created these monsters and dragons, and perhaps it is through conscientious and creative storytelling with children that we can learn to undo what we have mistakenly created.

For information about *The Sorcerer's Apprentice* visit:
http://press.princeton.edu/titles/10942.html

Gathering at the Well

TAFFY THOMAS MBE

The following piece is based on a keynote speech I delivered to the Annual Gathering of the Society for Storytelling at Oundle in 2011, a year after becoming the First Laureate for Storytelling.

For the following 750 or so words please accept the metaphor that there is a well that contains all the stories, myths and legends that have been told since the 'Big Bang', and all the skills needed to pass them on, for they only survive by being told from one friend to another.

Everyone, adult or child, battling to achieve literacy has had to make their way to that well, for as I have learned, '*You can't write a story unless you can tell a story, and you can't tell a story unless you've heard a story.*'

Teachers and educators are enriched by a visit to the well, but for anyone involved in pastoral work it is essential. For as poet Ben Okri wrote:

> It is easy to forget how mysterious and mighty stories are. They do their work in silence, invisibly. They work with all the internal materials of the mind and self. They become part of you while changing you. Beware the stories you read or tell; subtly, at night, beneath the waters of consciousness, they are altering your world.

One of the first literary figures to visit the well in 1386 then hosted the first ever English Storytelling circle in a pub, somewhere along the way on a pilgrimage to Canterbury, was Chaucer. He deemed the tales to be of such worth that he saw them committed to print. Many notable authors and playwrights feature folkloric narrative in their acclaimed works, including Hardy, Dickens, Rowling and indeed Shakespeare himself, and that's only some of the British ones. There is probably great value in all of us calling at the well, for as the life force that was Terry Pratchett once wrote, 'People think that stories are shaped by people. In fact, it's the other way around.'

I myself had to make my way to the well at the age of 35, albeit limping, as I survived a massive stroke that cost me the use of my left side and indeed my speech. The structures of the folk tales I found helped to heal my damaged brain, and speaking them breathed life into my then slurred and monotone speech patterns.

With the music of speech being the tool of fine storytellers, it is not surprising that many composers, both classical and contemporary, made their way to the well. There Offenbach discovered Orpheus in the Underworld. Britten found the tale of Peter Grimes on the Suffolk Salt Marshes. More recently Bob Dylan, Paul Simon and Lennon and McCartney have put tunes to a wealth of rich narratives.

I have long believed that oral storytelling is not so much a literary art as a visual art, albeit a virtual one, the teller and the tale creating an image in the mind of the listener. From this standpoint, it is not surprising that all over the world visual artists have been inspired to create works of great beauty from stories garnered at the well.

Native artists from the Americas and the Antipodes mark their culture and their history with images from their stories on bark, skin, parchment and rock. Storytellers have long told tales where heroes like Jack or St George battled successfully with the devil or a dragon as the personification of evil. These stories of good versus evil have long been the images many artists have used in their iconic paintings. Painters from Bosch to Blake famously depicted this battle. All these artists must have visited the well.

They probably queued up alongside philosophers and politicians such as Churchill, who definitely drew from the well for his witty narrative. Also queuing are comedians such as Dave Allen and Billy Connolly, born storytellers.

Yet remember that all of these great storytellers, whatever their discipline, upon visiting the well learned that just as important as gathering the stories was developing the ability to listen, for as I always say, '*If speaking was more important than listening we'd have two tongues and one ear.*'

Any person who strives to make the world a better place with the help of stories during their short lifespan has been at the well, for as I have come to believe, '*Storytelling preserves the past, reveals the present and creates the future.*'

So wait no longer, join the queue to be entertained, educated and enriched. Then you too can entertain, educate and enrich the lives of those dear to you.

Word Magic

HUGH LUPTON

What is it that speech does?

We are told that 'In the Beginning was the Word'. Whether by 'the Word' we mean the 'Big Bang' that set the universe in motion, or the breath of the divine 'logos' doesn't matter. The truth implicit in the statement is that vibration is at the core of creation. Without it there would be nothing.

When we speak we echo that first act of creation. With each of our utterances we create the world anew. Using a repertoire of sounds that are drawn from the environment that surrounds us – mediated through the breath, the lips and the tongue – each of our utterances sings the world into being a second time. Speech is a pattern of symbolic sound that can name, describe and animate – but is not bound to the environment that inspires it.

It has an independent life. It conjures a parallel world, a secondary world.

In his poem 'Full Moon and Little Frieda', Ted Hughes describes a 'cool small evening shrunk to a dog bark and the clank of a bucket'. His little daughter is with him. She is attentive in the way that only small children can be: 'And you listening. A spider's web, tense for the dew's touch.' Cows are going home in the lane 'looping the hedges with their warm wreaths of breath.' Then, out of the solemn ordinary evening, the child's utterance comes:

> 'Moon!' you cry suddenly, 'Moon! Moon!'
> The moon has stepped back like an artist gazing amazed at a work
> That points at him amazed.[1]

I don't know the circumstances of 'Full Moon and Little Frieda'. I like to think that Frieda had been shown the moon from her bedroom window. Maybe she had seen it in picture books and on walks. She must have heard the word spoken over and over. And now, for the first time, in the presence of this full moon, she shapes the sound herself, with lips and breath and tongue, and she utters it: 'Moon'.

And the moon is not indifferent. Like an artist he gazes amazed 'at a work that points at him amazed'. There is a reciprocity between the named and the namer.

The moon sees himself coming to life on the breath of the little girl who speaks his name. He is like a creator, Pygmalion perhaps, seeing his creation, his name-sake, taking on a life of its own.

And this is what will happen. Frieda will take the new word with her. It will become independent of the real moon. In the daytime she will be able to speak its sound and conjure the moon into being. She will be able to play with it. She will be able to say, 'I have hidden the moon under my hat,' and the real moon will have no power to contradict her.

This is where stories begin, in that parallel, secondary world.

Where does the word 'Moon' come from? It is derived from the Old English 'Mona', which in turn is derived from the Proto Germanic 'Menon' (also the source of Danish 'maane', German 'mond') and 'Menon' is derived from the Indo-European word 'menses' meaning both month and moon.

When Frieda pressed her lips together to make the mmm sound and followed it with the breath of a vowel, she was shaping the sound that countless generations have used to name the mysterious orb that circles the night sky. If we listen beyond the Indo-European root, we can hear the echoes of whatever language was spoken by our Palaeolithic ancestors.

Spoken words give us the power to name, to animate, to describe. They give us the power to loosen the bonds of experience, to take the given world and recreate it as sound, as speech and song.

In Norse mythology there is a dialogue between Thor and a dwarf called Alvis:

Thor: What is the moon called, that men see,
In all the worlds there are?'

Alvis: 'Moon' by men, 'The Ball' by gods,
'The Whirling Wheel' in Hel's realm,
'The Speeder' by giants, 'The Bright One' by dwarves,
By elves 'The Tally of Years'.[2]

When did the naming begin? Studies have been made of vervet monkeys showing that they have a repertoire of vocalisations. Many are used to warn of predators. There is a 'leopard call', a 'snake call', an 'eagle call'. They also use sounds to communicate emotion. But none of these sounds can be abstracted from the experience or mood itself. The utterances are tied to the moment and have no autonomy. A vervet monkey cannot articulate 'eagle' unless there's an eagle present. He cannot articulate 'anger' unless he is angry. Primatologists have found that much the same is true of all the 'great apes'.

Scholars are still arguing about why and how early man developed the capacity for symbolic language, for words that had a life independent of the event. Was it (as Noam Chomsky suggests) a sudden single chance mutation in the brain of one early man or woman that made possible an innate capacity for a 'grammar', giving him or her a genetic advantage that – over many generations – became dominant? Or was it a very slow evolution over millions of years from primate vocalisation, through gesture, facial expression and tool-making (coupled with the changing shape of the larynx) that culminated in speech?

We will probably never know. The one thing scholars do agree is that by the Middle Stone Age in Africa, *Homo sapiens* were using red ochre pigment for ritual and symbolic purposes, and would – by that time – have had a corresponding symbolic language not dissimilar in its complexity to ours. Certainly, by the time our ancestors migrated from Africa and began to populate the world (about 100,000 years ago) they were talking, and among their vocalisations would have been a sound that symbolized 'Moon'.

In every culture there is a fascination with the question of whether there could be a reciprocity between the spoken word and the actual thing its sound symbolizes. A word has the power to invoke an image in the mind's eye, but could it also invoke the thing itself? This is the territory of incantations, spells and curses. The magician's spell 'Abracadabra' has its origin in the Hebrew 'Abra-ke-ad-ebra', which can be translated as 'I create what I speak'. In mythic accounts of the early times there is often a fluidity between the name, the namer and the named. An Inuit woman is recorded as saying:

In the very earliest time
when people and animals lived on the earth,
a person could become an animal if he wanted to
and an animal could become a human being.
Sometimes they were people
and sometimes animals
and there was no difference.

All spoke the same language.
That was a time when words were like magic.
The human mind had mysterious powers.
A word spoken by chance
might have strange consequences.
It would suddenly come alive
and what people wanted to happen could happen –
all you had to do was say it.
Nobody could explain this:
That's the way it was.[3]

There is a sense of that fluidity in the following story from Siberia, which seems to carry traces of ancient belief.

There was once a herdsman who had a beautiful daughter. She was so beautiful that the Moon looked down from the sky and desired her.

One day she was out on the open snow with one of her reindeer. The reindeer looked up and saw that the Moon was getting larger. He blinked and looked again. The Moon was riding down from the sky in his sledge that was drawn by two sky reindeer.

'Look out!' he said. 'The Moon is coming down. He will seize you and carry you up into the sky.'

'What shall I do?'

The reindeer dug a hole in the snow with his hooves.

'Jump in!'

He kicked the snow on top of her until only her hair showed, like grass that snow had not covered.

The Moon leapt from his sledge.

'Where is she?'

He searched but could not find her.

'I'll be watching. When she re-appears, I will take her and enjoy her.'

He rode back into the sky.

The girl scrambled out of the snow. She and the reindeer ran back to her father's tent. He was away. There was no one to protect her.

'What shall I do now?'

The reindeer said: 'Say "pounding-stone" and you will become one.'

The girl shook her head. 'No, the Moon will know me.'

'Say "hammer" and you will become one.'

'No, he will know me.'

'Say "tent pole" and you will become one.'

'He will know me.'

'Say "hair" and you will become a single hair on the hide that hangs across the doorway.'

'Even then he will know me.'

'Say "tallow lamp".'

'Yes! Then he will not discover me.'

So the girl said: 'Tallow lamp.'

Where she had been standing there was a tallow lamp flickering on the floor of the tent.

At that moment the hide door was torn open. In came the Full Moon. He searched the tent. He turned everything upside down. He searched high and low. But such was the strength of his light that he didn't notice the little tallow lamp flickering on the floor (when the moon shines we do not see the candle). Bellowing with rage he strode out of the tent and leapt into his sledge. He shook the reins and drove his reindeer up into the sky.

But the girl was clever, and she had a plan. She turned back into herself and ran out across the snow. She waved her arms: 'Here I am! Here I am!'

The moon whipped his reindeer round and galloped down again. He rushed into the tent: 'Where is she?'

But he could not see the tallow lamp.

He returned to his sledge. As soon as he was in the sky she ran out again.

'Here I am!'

He came down and entered the tent. The girl could see he was thinner and weaker than before.

Again and again she called him back.

Each time he was thinner.

When he was too weak to climb back into his sledge the girl knew she need not fear him any longer.

She ran out of the tent and seized him. She bound him with leather thongs and threw him down onto the snow.

He looked up at her. He was trembling.

'You can kill me now if you want to. But if you find it in your heart to set me free then I will serve you and your people until the end of time.'

'How will you help us?'

'My light will guide you and give you pleasure. It will turn night into day over the white snow. And I will become the measure of the year.'

'Tell me more.'

'First I will be the Moon of the Old Reindeer Song,

then I will be the Moon of Bitter Cold Udders,

then the Moon of Full Udders,

then the Moon of New-Born Reindeer Calves,

then the Moon of Water,

then the Moon of First Leaves,

then the Moon of Warm Weather,

then the Moon of Shedding Antlers,

then the Moon of Light Frost,

then the Moon of Pairing Reindeer,

then the Moon of the Reindeer's Winter Back,

then the Moon of Shorter Days.'

The girl shook her head.

'But if I set you free you will grow fat and strong again. You'll carry me up into the sky.'

'No. I can see you are too clever for me. I will never come down again.'

The girl untied him. She rubbed fat into his skin where the leather knots had chafed him. She helped him into his sledge. He shook the reins and his reindeer galloped into the sky.

And the Moon was true to his word. He became each month in turn. He became the measure of the years. And whenever he grows fat and strong and looks down and desires a woman of the world, he remembers the girl and finds himself growing weaker.[4]

To tell a story is to engage with the secondary act of creation.

Our raw materials are the repertoire of sounds that have come down to us from remote history. They are the sounds that have been formalised and ordered into 'mother tongue'. They have reached us orally from earliest childhood. They are the deep language of thought and feeling. They are the sonic patterns we have used to make sense of the world.

Each word has its own life, its particular energy.

Moon. MOON.

When the word is set down on page or screen, what we see is a cipher. The living thing has been fettered by the traces of typeset.

If we close our eyes and speak the word aloud (like Little Frieda) it begins to sing. It begins to conjure itself into being.

That is why the first law of storytelling is that the stories should be spoken and heard, not read or even read aloud.

If a story is 'learned by heart' (and not by rote), the teller is forced to bypass the written forms that dominate our culture and allow the language its full resonance and history. As Alan Garner has written, 'not phonetics, grammar and syntax, but pitch and cadence and the colour of the word.'[5]

The storyteller has a role as a 'minder' of language. We must be respectful and careful with our inheritance. It is not a toolkit but another world that must be treated with care. Everything that is in our world is in that world. And just as our own primary world can be secularised and drained of mystery by a shabby materialism, so can the secondary world that words inhabit. The two are not unconnected.

What does it mean for a storyteller to honour the word?

Firstly, a wide vocabulary is essential. A word-hoard that draws from dialect words, slang words, from Chaucer and Shakespeare, from ballad and popular song, from translations of the oral and epic poetries of the world. The list could go on. The wider the net can be thrown the deeper and richer the resource.

Secondly the storyteller must work on his or her voice. There are no rules about this, and every voice is true to itself. But if the voice is to carry the word it must be audible, it must be paced so that the words are able to do their conjuring work. It all begins with the breath. In Greek the word for breath is '*zoe*', it is also the word for life. The breath that blows through us is the source of our life. It is also the source of our sounding. It carries the vowels that are broken by lips, tongue and teeth into language. The breath is driven from the belly. The bellows that drive it are rooted in the solar plexus. It is from here that we draw the energy to sustain a story. The storyteller's work on his or her voice is a long process of experiment.

Thirdly the storyteller must understand that to speak is also to sing. Every utterance, every sounding, is tuneful. Speech follows the rules of song, it rides on rhythm, its inflections and cadences are melodies.

Fourthly the storyteller must see what he is describing. If the teller, in his mind's eye, can visualise a word, can make it into image, then his audience will see it too. This is the deep meaning of 'imagination'.

Lastly the storyteller must understand the limits of the word. Beyond what we can see with our eyes and imagine with our mind's eye, beyond what we can identify and name, beyond moon, sun, sky, stars, water, earth and stone is mystery. Beyond primary and secondary worlds is mystery. Beyond creation is mystery: the mystery of our being here, alive, in this moment. Words and stories circle round this mystery, try to give it form, but finally it is beyond words. It is the storyteller's role to consciously live inside this paradox.

There was once a shopkeeper. A bag was sitting on the counter of his shop. A stranger came into the shop and started bargaining for one thing and then another. Suddenly he picked up the bag, tucked it under his arm and walked out of the shop. It was as if it had belonged to him since the day he was born.

The shopkeeper ran out into the street and grabbed the stranger's cloak: 'Stop thief! That bag and all that's in it, belongs to me!'

The stranger began to struggle, the shopkeeper shouted for help.

Soon there was a crowd. They seized the stranger and pinned him to the ground.

'Bring this scoundrel before the judge, and he will hear my complaint against him.'

Immediately willing hands helped the shopkeeper drag the stranger before the judge. But before he had time to open his mouth the stranger shouted: 'Allah, increase the power of our judge. This bag is my bag and all that is in it belongs to me. I lost it, and then found it again on this man's counter.'

'When did you lose it?' asked the judge.

'Yesterday, and I could not sleep for thinking about it.'

'In that case,' said the judge, 'tell me what is in the bag.'

Without a moment's hesitation the stranger answered: 'Oh judge, there are in the bag two lemonade glasses with gilded rims, a handkerchief, one large knitting needle, a pregnant cat, two beds, one large water jar, two racing camels, a palace with two reception halls, two burning torches and my entire family all ready to swear that the bag is my bag.'

Then the judge turned to the shopkeeper: 'What answer have you to this?'

'May Allah lift up and honour our noble judge,' he replied. 'I know that in my bag there are two dog kennels, a fishing net, a shepherd's crook, a blacksmith's furnace, two jolly fellows playing dice, a ruined pavilion, an army with its captains, the city of Baghdad and a thousand monks all ready to bear witness that this bag is my bag.'

When the stranger heard this, he burst into tears: 'Oh, our master judge, the bag is known to be mine and mine only. Besides those things I've mentioned before it also contains four chess players, a mare and two foals, a linen cloak, a ship with all its sailors, ten fortified cities, a blind man, a lame man, two green tents and a thousand saints all ready to swear that this bag is my bag!'

The judge turned the shopkeeper again. 'What answer do you have to that?'

'May Allah make strong the judgement of our noble judge. I should add that as well as those trifles already mentioned, there are in my bag gardens filled with trees and flowers, a newly married couple with their marriage fresh about them, a black man playing a clarinet, the palace of Solomon, a nail, a plank, the whole of India, twenty chests filled with silk, a coffin, a thousand bull elephants, twelve disgraceful farts, a full moon, two turbans and a razor to shave the beard of the judge if he does not recognise that the bag is mine!'

When the judge had heard all this, he looked them both up and down: 'Either you are a pair of rascals making a mockery of the law, or else this bag is a bottomless pit and a wonder to end all wonders.'

And to see which one had spoken the truth the judge opened the bag. He opened it in the full view of the whole watching crowd… and he found inside it a piece of dried orange peel and three olive stones.

At once the shopkeeper shook his head: 'This bag is certainly not mine! It must indeed belong to that lying scoundrel of a stranger!'

He turned on his heel and walked back to his shop.

The stranger took the bag, tucked it under his arm and turned in the other direction.

He was never seen again.

One of the shopkeeper's neighbours followed him home: 'Friend, why did you let the stranger win so easily? Now you've lost the bag. You were the loser in that contest and he was the winner.'

The shopkeeper spat on the ground.

'Not at all. For in the minds of that crowd my bag will always be full of wonders. His will never contain more than a piece of orange peel and three olive stones.'[6]

Notes

1   From 'Full Moon and Little Frieda', from *Wodwo*, Ted Hughes, Faber & Faber, 1967.

2   From 'The Words of the All-Wise', from *The Elder Edda*, Paul B. Taylor and W.H. Auden (trans.), Faber & Faber, 1973.

3   'Magic Words', from *Symposium of the Whole*, D. Rothenberg (ed.), University of California Press, 1983.

4   Siberian folk tale adapted from 'The Moon and Time' in *The Moon, Myth and Image*, Jules Cashford, Cassell, 2003.

5   From the Introduction to Alan Garner's *Book of British Fairy Tales*, Collins, 1984.

6   Adapted from *The Thousand Nights and One Night*, J.C. Mardrus & P. Mathers (trans.), Routledge & Keegan Paul, 1972.

Telling the Mabinogi

MICHAEL HARVEY

Anyone can tell a story and tell it well. We do it socially all the time and many of the techniques that work well in formal storytelling situations are embedded in our social storytelling, where the appeal of the story is such that we are pulled into the material to the extent that we are not aware of how it is done – perhaps the hallmark of any artform done well.

And what are these hidden skills? Well, the clearly articulated difference between action, description, dialogue, information and comment for a start. And then there's the ability to regulate the degree of physical embodiment we use, the incorporation of character, the complexity of gaze

and interaction with the audience to name but a few things – and in our social storytelling we don't even know we are doing it!

However, once we try to work on material that is not social, not part of our direct experience or family or community history, things become more complicated and we are faced with the central problem of the contemporary storyteller: 'How do I get material that is outside myself, inside myself so I can tell with authenticity and conviction?' In order to start to answer that question it is important to become conscious of the social storytelling skills in order to reapply them to this new material.

The Material

There are many varied methods of doing this and for this article I just want to look at how the job can be done when working with mythic material, specifically the Mabinogion, a collection of Welsh stories probably first written down sometime in the twelfth or thirteenth century. The material represents part of the repertoire of the 'cyfarwydd', or medieval court storyteller, and the style of the stories clearly demonstrates their oral origins. The stories are divided into those that bear the echoes of pre-history (the Four Branches of the Mabinogi and Culhwch and Olwen) and the Four Romances, which have a more medieval flavour, and here I will be concentrating on the earlier material, specifically the Fourth Branch of the Mabinogi in the form of the show 'Dreaming the Night Field', developed and toured with Adverse Camber Productions.

In this story we have an intense mix of magic, transformation, trickery, war, rape, devotion and nurturing without much context or orientation, and at first meeting the stories are challenging in their form because we are not the intended audience and do not have the mindset or cultural references of medieval Welsh courtly society. We are not given the benefit of a clear linear narrative but have to cope with plot holes, seemingly random magical events and untold backstories. But still the stories pull us

in and invite us outside the lines of the books they are written in, into a wider weave of landscape and parallel texts.

Storied Landscape

Treated as a self-contained narrative the stories can appear disconcerting and disorientating, but looking more closely at the text there are clear signposts into the actual, living landscape of Wales that can help root and focus our attention as we grapple with the material. Many Welsh traditional stories have a direct and intimate connection with specific landscapes and none more than the Fourth Branch, where there are a number of locations that you can visit today that are not that different to how they would have been when the stories were being told by the 'cyfarwyddiaid' of the Welsh court. The locations are too many to mention here but amongst them there is Llech Ronw (the Stone of Gronw), behind which the character Gronw Pebr hid to shelter from the spear blow of the enraged Lleu Llaw Gyffes at the end of the story. Incredibly, the stone was only discovered just over twenty years ago in the area where the story happened. It is surrounded by three smallholdings whose names still bear witness to the spear blow and the man who was killed.

Standing in front of the stone is a strange and wonderful experience with the frisson that the story actually happened here; however, it has none of the feel of a crime scene or a simple piece of evidence. There is a constellation of stone, river, hole and the surrounding smallholdings, whose names form a dynamic weave around the stone so that we seem to step out of the linearity of event time into a wider weave. Wide indeed when you consider that several of the characters in this story are linked with specific constellations and that some of the backstories also connect us with Annwn, the Welsh Otherworld, lying in a parallel layer of reality 'under' ours.

Making the Show

Actually, making the piece started with a joint commitment to work on this material and a joint expression as a group and individuals of what made us want to tell it. Then we assembled the material, visited the sites, collected parallel texts, music and songs, and wrestled with the question of scenography. We got other artists involved to help us with vocal improvisation and deepen our contact with story and location, spent time in residence in the Felin Uchaf Centre in North Wales, and gradually started showing our work to critical friends and communities of practice until we were ready for our preview at Beyond the Border in 2016 and premiere at Aberystwyth the following spring. The work was communal and shared, each of us focusing on our specialism but deliberately stepping out of our comfort zones to find new areas of learning and nudging one another out of our habitual patterns and safety zones.

The work of turning narrative into embodied experience so that we can tell with authenticity and spontaneity is one that individual storytellers do in their own ways, but I use a combination of all those elements that are hidden in plain sight in social telling plus a few others that I have picked up along the way, adapted from practitioners I admire and my time at the 3rd Labo experimental storytelling group at La Maison du Conte in Paris.

If I was to give anyone embarking on a project with similar material a piece of advice, I would say, 'Resist the temptation to rush in and fix things.' This will always give you a result that may look OK but will never be really inspiring, surprising or real. Instead, make clear, articulate interventions in the material and the process using the tools at your disposal – and only one at a time. The work is complex enough already and if we make our way in with clarity and an open mind our attention will seep in to the material and we will soon start to resonate with its complexity rather than merely illustrate it. The clunkiness that you are trying to fix is just part of the creative process and will soon disappear. Believe me, audiences will thank you for this.

Scenography

This was the first time we had worked with scenography in any really meaningful way and was one of the biggest and most satisfying challenges of making the piece. We decided against using a backdrop and instead use something more dynamic, and, after a lot of experimentation and collaboration with our designer, we decided to use sticks that could take on a number of configurations during the show. We attempted to avoid illustration but wanted to change the dynamic on stage to allow the audience to see new shapes and make more associations.

Projection of meaning, feeling and intention onto and into the performance environment is common in storywalks, where nature seems to uncannily participate in the telling, and we wanted to bring the same phenomenon into our building-based work. We wished to avoid privileging the performance space over and above the auditorium as, for us, it is important that the audience and ourselves share the same space, as we would on a storywalk. To achieve this, we are present as ourselves as the audience comes in and the musicians sing, as themselves, before the lighting state goes into show mode. As the audience enters, about half the sticks are in the auditorium and are moved into the space as the show opens.

Contemporary Intrusions

We are also part of the process. Culturally and personally we bring things into the room and we are affected by the material and enter into a creative resonance with it. Our own impressions of the site and the details of what we saw are woven into the introduction of the piece and even things that seem, at first sight, to clash with the story, like the nuclear power station that dominates the view from Tomen y Mur, site of much of the action in the Fourth Branch, become prescient and resonant when we remember the undoable nature of the dangerous magic employed in the story. A premeditated rape is an essential part of the development of the plot

and a cascade of events that make up the first half of the show. In the story the victim has a few words of dialogue with the king before justice is administered, but we wanted to pay more attention to this moment and worked on presenting this using an adapted section of the 2016 Stanford University sexual assault victim impact statement. This was a bold decision and had to be worked on so that it felt true, appropriate and strong enough.

Performing the Show

Improvisation is a central part of what we do. Yes, the same things happen to the same people in the same order each time and the same songs are sung, but within that framework we are always looking for how it is going to be different tonight. The lack of script means that the precise verbal form and emphasis of presentation is different for each audience and the music and singing also have a corresponding intuitive and spontaneous responsiveness. Even our technician is deftly tweaking lights and sound as we go along.

A lot of planning and preparation has gone into the moment of being ready to go on stage and once we are in front of the audience it is the time to trust that the planning has been done properly, trust that we are ready and that this particular show will work into a version that resonates and sings with the space and the audience, and trust that the material will, once again, weave its spell over those who tell and those who listen.

Credits, Links and Sources

'Dreaming the Night Field' is an Adverse Camber Production with Michael Harvey (story), Stacey Blythe (music) and Lynne Denman (song), with Paula Crutchlow (dramaturg) and Sophia Clist (design).
www.adversecamber.org
www.michaelharvey.org

Articles

'Staging the Story' by Michael Harvey (http://bit.ly/stagingthestory)

Books

Davies, Sioned, *The Mabinogion*, OUP, 2008

Ifans, Dafydd and Rhiannon, *Y Mabinogion*, Gomer, 2001

Williams, Ifor, *Pedeir Keinc y Mabinogi*, Gwasg Prifysgol Cymru, 1994

Storytelling for the Very Young

ANNE E. STEWART

I'll never forget Mem Fox telling 'The Little Match Girl' to a group of librarians and teachers in Darwin early on in my storytelling career. I remember the tears in my eyes, the sadness, and the lump in my throat; she had us all there, eating out of the palm of her hand. Not a loud theatrical Mem but rather a quiet reflective Mem in keeping with the emotions of the story. What power, what a storyteller! But more than that, there was one thing in particular that has always stayed with me. Mem has a tremendous appreciation and passion for stories, language and literacy. Telling stories, she explained, is like the pouring forth of precious jewels: each delicious

word to be savoured, to be handed to children with love, respect, passion and reverence.

Fifteen years on, with countless pre-school storytimes under my belt, I too have a passionate belief in the importance of developing in children a love of language and literature. I still thrill to the eager upturned faces that look at me adoringly. I always know when I've told stories to a child, even if I don't remember their face. They look at me like we are old friends, like we've shared adventures together. But of all the age groups, pre-schoolers are probably the trickiest, the most intense, the most constant. There is no chance to relax into a long story. Pre-school sessions necessarily move along at a fast pace, moving from rhyme to story to song. Pre-schoolers have no qualms about showing you their cut finger in the middle of the story, or telling you their cat's name or what they had for breakfast. It's hard work. However, telling pre-schoolers stories and creating a love for the magic and music of words is probably one of our most important jobs.

Fifteen years on, I have learnt many tricks and developed a quiet confidence in my abilities and the stories I have chosen to work with. This article purports to share some of these with you. Nothing can beat experience when it comes to the art of storytelling, but some guidelines help start you on the path. I have always found it easier to work with themes with pre-school storytimes, be it as simple as food, the wind, animals or bath time, it helps me to focus the session and find material from the excellent plethora of stories, songs and rhymes available. The trick is to work up a package that incorporates a range of material. Let me give you some examples. Ann Pellowski in her excellent book *The Story Vine* has a simple version of 'How the Years were Named for the Animals'.

A beautiful old Chinese story starts with the Buddha sitting under his sacred Bodhi Tree. Let's take this as a starting point for exploring pre-school storytelling. I saw Pellowski tell this story using twelve tiny animal figurines. At the time I couldn't find any myself, so I cut out and pasted the animals in the story on to black cardboard. They were big and bold and young children quickly got the idea to name the animals with me as the story progressed. First year the rat, second year the ox, third year the tiger, fourth year the rabbit, fifth year the dragon and so on. Let's start with the year of the rat. First some nursery rhymes, 'Hickory Dickory Dock, the mouse ran up the clock. Okay everyone, arms up nice and straight, so we can watch your little mice run up them.' With these developing listeners it is a good idea to involve them with action rhymes, get them to join in in a focused way. During my time working in libraries, Elisabeth Matterson's *This Little Puffin* was always in my reference collection, a well-organised great source for nursery rhymes and appropriate actions. With this early age group, I invariably use lots of props. 'I've brought some visitors to meet you today, they're very small and very shy and frightened of cats. Can you guess what they are?' Out of my pocket I produce two little mice (available from pet shops as toys for cats). 'These are my friends Tom Thumb and Hunka Munka, they want to do a little poem with you. Now because you haven't got any mice, maybe you'd like to pretend with me. Put your hand out flat and pretend it's a nest and use your pointer and middle finger of the other hand as mice.' Now: Two little mice sat down to spin. Pussy passed by, and popped his head in. What are you doing my little men? We're weaving coats for gentlemen. Can I come in and bite off the thread? No, no Pussy, you'd bite off our heads.' I'll then repeat this through the session. This poem then naturally leads to a longer story, *Two Bad Mice* by Beatrix Potter. All of this takes about twenty minutes, quite long enough for beginning listeners. If your pre-schoolers are well trained and it's later in the year, you could extend it by searching for related stories.

Working in a library I was always on the lookout for new material, but if you don't, try looking for a reference book titled *Subject Access to Picture Books*, this could save you hours of perusing the shelves. Let's pick some more animals from our Chinese Years, say the Rooster and the Dragon, my Chinese animal and my daughter's respectively. I love telling this story and children seem to really concentrate on it. 'The Rooster and the Heavenly Dragon' can be found in a multicultural collection by Margaret Read MacDonald. 'Once, the rooster had beautiful golden horns on the top of his head,' and so it goes. In my hometown of Daylesford, in Victoria, Australia, I earn my bread and butter money at a shop called 'Dragons and

Dreaming'. Three metres of scaly red dragon wraps itself around the wall protecting a small cave where I tell stories.

Naturally I've got a lot of dragon lore. You must hunt out Jack Prelutsky's book of dragon poems *The Dragons are Singing Tonight* – the title poem is sensational and I love sharing beautiful rhythmic poetry like this. Would you believe I've even adapted P.D. Eastman's classic *Are you my Mother?*, to 'Are yee me kinfolk?' I gathered all the props from my children's toys together with a handsome green Sri Lankan Dragon puppet I had. It's like this: Mother dragon goes off to look for food. While she's gone her baby in its egg is washed down into a deep dark lake. Claws start scratching and the baby dragon emerges to look for his mother. He finds out he's not a fish that has scales like him and he's not a reptile with claws like his, and not a bird that can fly or a fire that burns. He wanders back to his nest and his mother finds him. How deliciously satisfying for a child, to be back home with his mother who loves him. I've even got a version featuring dinosaurs! Year of the Snake leads me to several other favourite books, poems and stories.

Once again I recommend Anne Pellowsk's *The Story Vine*, this time for its string tricks. I had the great fortune to meet Ann and collected a few of her stories and tricks. I have employed poetic license and changed her snake into Gorialla the Rainbow serpent; I also do the mosquito trick. While on an aboriginal theme, I have also adapted an action rhyme Pellowski illustrates in her book. My niece, Esther, was called Muk Muk by the aboriginal people of central Australia, where she was born, because of her big round eyes like an owl. The actions are in the book, but this is how I tell it, once children have guessed that Muk Muk is an aboriginal word for owl.

Muk Muk sat in the branch of a tree, as quiet as quiet can be. It was night and her eyes were open like this. She looked all around – not a thing did she see. Two mice started creeping up the trunk of the tree and they stopped below the branch, to see what they could see. The solemn old owl said 'Twooit Twoooh.' Up jumped the mice and down they flew.

I always have great fun with another aboriginal story, that of Tiddalick the giant frog that drinks up all of the water. I have a big green balloon that I blow up as Tiddalick drinks up all the water and gets fatter and fatter and bigger and bigger. I love the children's nervous trepidation, will it or won't it burst? I tell the version from the ABC book *Favourite Playschool Stories* or maybe it's in the collection *More Favourite Playschool Stories*, whatever; I recommend you get them both. Likewise, the *Playschool Useful Book* is a must for those interested in developing pre-school themes. A list could go on and on about the stories, poems and rhymes that have become like old friends, but I should conclude with some practical aspects of pre-school storytelling.

Interruptions: I'm afraid these will always happen no matter how experienced you are or how well you know your stories. Don't let it phase you! Don't ignore the child or they'll keep badgering, but a firm 'You can tell me after the story' will help. We are training these young people in their listening skills, so we need to be pro-active. A couple of favourite lines that always work for me are: 'Do you know how I can tell children are ready for a story? They're sitting up nice and straight and looking at me,' and 'Oh dear, I can't go on, somebody's talking and that will spoil the story for everyone else,' then you eyeball the yapper. The stories you choose will stay in your repertoire for a long time so make sure they are stories you love. To hark back to Mem, you need to be passionate about your choices. Keep your storytime moving along, include a range of material, and vary the length of pieces you present. Children learning language love repetition so make sure you include old favourites like The Gingerbread Boy, or the Hobyahs and invite the children to join in this structured way. Beware of opened-ended questions with the very young, their minds could be wandering anywhere and you may not get the response you had hoped for. Finally, to finish, a quote from another favourite storyteller of mine, Patricia Scott from Tasmania (who has won the Dromkeen Medal for her contribution to children's literature): 'Like your story, know your story. Relax and enjoy the telling.'

Suggested Reading

Bird, Bettina and Prentice, Jeffrey, *Dromkeen: A Journey into Children's Literature*, J.M. Dent, 1987

Colwell, Eileen, *Storytelling*, Bodley Head, 1980

Gillard, Marni, *Storyteller, Storyteacher: Discovering the Power of Storytelling for Teaching and Living*, Stenhouse, 1995

Pellowski, Anne, *The World of Storytelling*, H.W. Wilson, 1991

Perrow, Susan, *Healing Stories for Challenging Behaviour*, Hawthorn Press, 2008

Rosen, Betty, *And None of it Was Nonsense*, Scholastic, 1988

Saxby, Maurice, *Give Them Wings: The Experience of Children's Literature*, Macmillan, 1987

Shedlock, Marie L., *The Art of the Storyteller*, Dover, 2003

Yashinsky, Dan, *Suddenly They Heard Footsteps: Storytelling for the Twenty-First Century*, Vintage Canada, 2010

From Talebones

TONY COOPER

Firstly; I am, at heart and by occupation, a story*teller*. For the last thirty-odd years I have been used to indulging in live *two*-way communications as I tell stories from memory accompanied by a constant stream of reactions from the audiences as I tell. These reactions influence the way the story is told and mould it to the tastes and needs of that specific audience. The storytelling is interactive; rather in the way that a small stream flowing down to the sea across a beach of sand creates a winding path, then is itself influenced by the very path that it has created. The water moulds the flow through the sand, washing away here and depositing there to create the bends that in turn guide the water. In the

same way the story affects the audience whose reactions in turn influence the telling.

This writing business is horribly and rigidly one-way; from the author to the reader. There are no reactions from you to guide me how to proceed; no gasps, no groans, no smiles nor laughs. The computer word-processor occasionally chips in with a comment, usually complaining; 'This sentence has no verb' or 'This paragraph is too long'. I attached a cardboard smile to the bottom of the monitor screen when I was writing my first book but over the weeks it slowly sagged and became sardonic, so it had to be disposed of. Secondly; I am sure that most college or university graduates are not daunted by great thick slabs of prose – but I am. To me they smack of dry serious learning, interminable pointless assignments and damp classrooms. I'm the sort of idle chap who flicks though any book looking for simple descriptions, précis, diagrams, the answers page and easily accessible ideas to make my life easier. 'Questions and Answers' will break up the slabs, so to speak; not only for the reader but also for me, the writer.

Talebones

Talebones are my name for stories which have been stripped down to the bare plot to rid them of their location, nationality, historical context and other specifics. Imagine it as a quick sketch in crayon of a well-known classical painting, or a few notes whistled to give the theme of a concerto. They were developed from, originally, A4 double-sided sheets, each one describing four stories per side that could be divided by the students into four double-sided mini-sheets; very portable and with the intention that they should be thrown away once the story had been told a couple of times. To make the tales fit into this small space and yet still be of a font size that was readable, the stories had to be reduced to a bare minimum. This had the fortunate side effect of allowing the students to impose their *own* variables; culture, geography and other

details from their personal experiences and combine them with the reactions and responses of the listeners to create a subtly new version of an old tale that was tailored to suit a specific audience.

 Variables

All the variables are added, chosen and delivered automatically by you whenever you start telling stories without a written text. Minute changes in the audience's breathing, attentiveness, posture, facial expression, laughter, dilation of the pupils and more than a dozen other subconsciously received signals gently guide the teller to choose the right words and how to use them. We were unthinkingly noticing these changes and acting upon them even when we were babies; in order to survive the rigours of infancy and childhood we very quickly learned to 'read' these tiny clues to other people's thoughts. In adulthood they are still there but they are as undetectable and as commonplace as water is to a fish; they are the interpersonal social medium in which we are all immersed. We don't stop responding to them as adults – they are just unconsciously used in everyday life to help us to respond appropriately in interactions with others. We only notice these clues to how to respond to other people when they are absent; we treat those who are unresponsive as anti-social or as being on the autistic spectrum.

Oral storytelling is probably the oldest teaching technique in the world. I am sure that Mr and Mrs *Homo Erectus* had amusing mime-tales about hunting, seeing off intruders and how one day Mr *Erectus* sat on the hot fire embers; these would have been both entertaining and instructive for their children and neighbours. *Aesop's Fables* and the parables of Jesus are probably the best known instructive stories in the Western world although others, like Sufi teaching tales featuring the idiot/wiseman Mulla Nasrudin, have become better known over the last fifty years. Jataka stories from India, Zen koans from Japan and Hasidic tales from the Jewish faith are other well-known story collections that are widely used sources of wisdom.

Stories are the way we **store information** in the brain. They help us to connect facts with other facts and organise the information. As Jane Yolen, editor of *Favourite Folktales from around the World*, explains: 'Storytelling, the oldest of arts, has always been both an entertainment and a cultural necessity. Storytellers breathed life into human cultures.'

Oral storytelling is an **emotional event**; tales go straight to the heart, creating a positive attitude towards the learning process. Whilst it is entirely possible to teach science, mathematics, astronomy and other 'hard-edged' subjects without cracking a smile or evoking a tear, the involvement resulting from a story well told will touch the heart and generate empathy and understanding.

Storytelling, with the powerful aspect of interactivity, develops **listening skills**. If the students know that they are soon to be asked to reproduce the tale that they are hearing, either in speech or writing, they will quickly develop a critical ear that stores and analyses the story.

Storytelling is a powerful **humanising element** in an increasingly technological age. Compared with other media like the written word, television, radio or film, a tale told live is like a 'wholefood' with nothing taken out; other media is comparable to pre-digested commercial pap catering to an idea of 'universal taste'. Its unresponsive delivery grinds on whether the audience's reaction is good or bad; no 'audience figures' or 'ticket sales' have ever altered the content of a book or a major media production except as maybe a slight 're-edit' after a 'pre-release viewing'. Side notes written by book readers serve to do nothing but annoy subsequent readers. Stand-up comedy and street theatre are a couple of the few other entertainments that share immediate audience responses and feedback with storytelling.

To quote major experts on the subject:

'The folk tale is the primer of the picture language of the soul.'

Joseph Campbell

'Stories, which rely so much on words, offer a major and constant source of language experience for children.'

Andrew Wright

'The primary reason to recommend storytelling in the classroom is that stories are motivating and immensely interesting, they can best attract listeners and promote communication. The excitement and drama of storytelling provide a context that holds students' attention.'

Robert B. Cooter

'Storytelling … costs nothing, is enjoyable, and can be used anywhere and at any time.'

M.K. Zabel

'If history were taught in the form of stories, it would never be forgotten.'

Rudyard Kipling

'All stories teach, whether the storyteller intends them to or not. They teach the world we create. They teach the morality we live by. They teach it much more effectively than moral precepts and instructions.'

Philip Pullman

'Thus I rediscovered what writers have always known (and have told us again and again): books always speak of other books, and every story tells a story that has already been told.'

Umberto Eco, postscript to The Name of the Rose

'Now, before you make a movie, you have to have a script, and before you have a script, you have to have a story; though some avant-garde directors have tried to dispense with the latter item you'll find their work only at art theatres.'

Arthur C. Clarke, 2001: A Space Odyssey

'After nourishment, shelter and companionship, stories are the thing we need most in the world.'

Philip Pullman

'Thought flows in terms of stories – stories about events, stories about people, and stories about intentions and achievements. The best teachers are the best story tellers. We learn in the form of stories.'

Frank Smith

'It is the supreme art of the teacher to awaken joy in creative expression and knowledge.'

Albert Einstein

The quotes supporting stories as a learning tool are endless. In short, told stories are a natural, timeless and international way of stimulating learning.

Here is a teaching tale, on the subject of teaching tales, from Rona Leventhal in the USA:

Why Storytelling?

A long time ago in a faraway land, a boy went to learn at the feet of a wise man. Day after day the wise man told the boy stories. One day, the boy asked, 'Master, why do you always teach through stories? Would it not be faster to tell me directly?' The wise man answered, 'Please bring me some tea.' The boy rose and prepared a cup of tea. He held the small cup gently in his hands as he carried it to the teacher. The wise man took the cup from the boy and sipped it, then asked, 'Why did you bring me a cup when I only asked for the tea?'

Rona writes:

When you hear a story together each member enters into a collective engagement of that story, of a journey, of community. The tales are universal, with their ability to touch people by expressing the whole

range of human experience and emotion. At the same time, the experience is personal, engaging the imagination and allowing people to understand underlying truths in a way that has staying power. Sometimes stories and their messages are familiar; other times it allows us to see the world through a different lens. Although every listener creates their own images, there is a shared collective experience. In this way, a storyteller binds an audience together, weaving the thread of the tale through each listener.

Storytelling is an ancient art form that has been used for centuries – long before the written word was created. It has been used as a teaching tool, as a source of cultural and local history and politics, as a form of persuasive argument, for knowledge sharing, to explain the natural world, in lieu of punishment, and of course, for entertainment. Stories are powerful, and effective tools for getting a message across or eliciting an emotional response...without preaching! Some of the best orators and educators are storytellers!

When students are involved with storytelling – as listeners, creators of stories or learning how to tell a story – they are (unwittingly) learning many skills while at the same time taking ownership of their stories. (www.ronatales.com)

Stories can sneak into the classroom for the most unusual reasons. I was once, surprisingly to me, a college lecturer in 'Sport, Leisure and Recreation Studies', about which I knew very little. My students were of various ages, but they had all joined the course through a common interest: sport. They were fit, well-muscled individuals with dark facial hair and gruff voices (the males in the group were even more so), who also shared a profound disinterest in reading and writing. They did, however, need to complete written assignments, so motivating them to produce work was a tricky business. One day the subject was the Health and Safety at Work Act 1974 and the ways in which it differed from the earlier Factories and Shops Act. I knew a straight lecture would have them asleep in a moment, so I prepared a cunning, if slightly theatrical, demonstration. After outlining the new Act and describing how responsibility for safety now rested on employees as well as the employers I produced two identical laboratory beakers each half full of a clear liquid. I told them that one contained pure water for me to drink but that the other contained concentrated acid for my ailing Ford Cortina car battery. I reminded them that since 1974, under the new Act my safety was their responsibility in that they represented employees as much as their safety was mine if I represented an employer. I also said that on the way down from the science department I had needed to put the beakers on the floor occasionally to open doors and that I was not entirely sure which beaker was water and which was acid. I continued to expound for around fifteen minutes then absent-mindedly moved to drink from one of the beakers. Several people screamed at me to stop. I reassured them that I knew that this was the water and confidently demonstrated the fact by stirring the fluid with a biro from my pocket. The biro promptly dissolved. More screaming from the students. Well, it was very warm water and the biro had been moulded from a clear Glacier Mint boiled sweet the night before. I then drank the liquid. Both the beakers contained water, of course. All the students passed their exams at the end of the year, even on boring content like the Health and Safety at Work Act 1974. I had made a tiny but memorable story of the basic concepts that were being taught.

How to Tell a Story from Memory

Perhaps it would be best to use a direct quote from a respected source of stories and how to tell them. The following is from the website 'Storyarts', created by New Yorker Heather Forest:

> The best way to improve storytelling skills is to *practice telling stories*. As your listeners travel into the tale with you, trust that your words will inspire their imaginations to conjure pictures. As those pictures become more

vivid, the storyteller fades into the background. Rather than wasting any energy on having stage fright or being self-conscious, truly give yourself over to telling your story. The more you inhabit your tale, the more listeners will be transported to the imaginary world you are creating for them and you, the teller, will virtually disappear. (www.storyarts.org/classroom/retelling/practice.html)

First of all you must really like the story that you are telling. This is more fundamental than it seems. To tell a tale that you find dull or obvious will tend to lead to an uninspired delivery; if you relish the story yourself then your enthusiasm will shine through. There are some stories that are so good that they seem to drive the teller to tell them to everyone as soon and as often as possible. The tales of 'Lazy Jack' and 'The Golden Spoon' were like that for me when first I started and they have stayed in my repertoire for more than thirty years. Stories that are as good as these are not rare, they are just tales that 'click' with the teller. I often remind the audience that I am only the last in a countless line of tellers of this tale stretching back through the ages, often into prehistory. If they like the story and they want to applaud they must remember that they are congratulating not only me the teller and the un-named creator who first created the tale in her mind, but also themselves, for without receptive listeners the whole exercise would be pointless.

The story telling consists of three interdependent elements: the story, the teller and the audience. These have been described by Doug Lipman, the American storyteller, as 'The Storytelling Triangle'. The relationships between these elements are of interest: Firstly, the teller has a relationship with the story; they found it, chose it for this occasion, understood or were intrigued by it and learned to tell it in their own way.

Secondly there is the relationship between the teller and the audience; they may be known to each other by reputation (for example 'Oh the Newtown crowd are hard to please' or 'She seems to dance through the

tale...') or by years of familiarity. Seasoned tellers have various ways of establishing a relationship with a new audience; some will start with a joke or a song or even sometimes a distinctive noise or an expression. There is much that can be usefully learned by storytellers from street performers or stand-up comedians

Thirdly, within this 'triangle' there is a relationship that you, as a storyteller, has very little control over which is the one between the audience and the story. Stories can be perceived by individuals in many different ways, rather like the group of blind men in Leo Tolstoy's tale who described an elephant as a leaf, a rope, a pillar, a tree, a wall and a weapon, depending on which part of the animal they had touched.

Relax. For many people the idea of appearing and speaking in front of a group of strangers can be intimidating. Controlling your breathing will help immensely. Take some slow deep breaths before you start. Try this technique from the Chinese Tai Chi exercises. When you have fully breathed in and first extended your stomach – breath in some more to expand your chest and fill your lungs completely. When you have breathed out as far as possible, first from the lungs and then from the stomach, blow a few puffs of air from between your lips to entirely empty out your lungs. Repeat the cycle around seven times; it has a calming influence. Yes, you may look ridiculous but the effect is worth it. Note: this is not to be done when driving or operating machinery; there is a small risk of hyperventilation. Singing or chanting also exercises and frees the lungs, the throat and larynx. Load up your car music system with favourite sing-along tracks and use that voice!

Start with something compelling to attract attention. Simply standing still and looking around at the audience with a confident smile sometimes works. If you seem to know what you are doing then the audience will be reassured that they will not be embarrassed on your behalf. Many traditional Caribbean tellers start with an 'audience response call' to ask for 'permission' to tell a tale. 'Crick!' you say, and they reply 'Crack!',

back and forth three times. This translates as 'I want to tell you a story!' and their reply, 'Tell us a story! We want to hear one!' This establishes a relationship between you and the audience and sets the tone for the whole session. I may sometimes appear to be dredging my mind for a suitable tale for these people and this occasion and then ask them a few questions, 'Do you know about the Queen who poisoned her own daughter?' or 'Do you know why the Isle of Thanet is called an "Isle" when it is firmly attached to Kent? Well, I was there and it happened like this…' I often begin by saying that one member of the audience is similar to a character in my story; for example:

> Queen Silvertree was the most beautiful woman in the land (much like… you! – if I may be so bold) although her beauty (unlike yours) was thanks to the art of the royal wigmaker, the steady hand of her make-up maid, and a couple of centipede skins whose legs doubled as lovely long eyelashes.

That 'pause' before the word 'you' is part of the well-known 'Pose/ Pause/Pounce' technique used by teachers everywhere to ensure that everyone momentarily considers the thought before relaxing when the victim has been chosen. (The teacher poses a question at large without asking any specific person, pauses while all the students consider the problem, then one person is asked for the answer.)

To my shame I have sometimes resorted to noisily cleaning out my ear with a finger (I have a toy squeaker concealed in my fist. I give many thanks to the Italian clown who showed me this one day in London's Covent Garden Market).

Troublesome or restless audiences I have experienced in the past have included sports students (as above with Health and Safety at Work Act 1974), nylon-clad Hello! reading ladies with precisely coiffured hair, young offenders craving tobacco, hyper-inactive rich children (who felt that as I was being paid I should do all the work) and middle management groups, especially the red-blooded 'sales teams' of a major company like

Nissan. All have yielded to the charm of a told tale. There is something about being told a story which encourages a relaxed yet attentive attitude from all people; from tiny tots to the elderly, from university professors to people with special learning needs.

Be audible. Your visual presentation, although it must be acceptable, fades into insignificance when compared with the effect of your prime tool; your voice. Speak initially to those at the back of the crowd. I often suggest to the audience that those who can't hear me should quietly scratch the back of their neck with their left ankle as a secret sign to me for higher volume. In reality good diction is probably more important than volume; an interested group will hear even a whisper. If you are brave record yourself telling a tale to someone else; you may be shocked, as I was, to discover that your voice is deeper or lighter than you thought. Likewise, regional accents are, in general, undetectable to ourselves. Being recorded on video also brings shocking revelations about facial expressions, weird mannerisms, posture, limb movements and dubious clothing choices. Audio and visual recordings may be painful to experience but there is no doubt that the self-knowledge is useful and is essential if we are to give full value as tellers.

Take your time. There is a tendency to be nervous and to hurry, which does few stories any good. A worried teller worries an audience. I have sometimes, in my early days of performing to large crowds, imagined that all these strangers in front of me have, at some time in the past, shared an exciting adventure with me or been a lover or a close friend. By this self-delusion all are perceived by me to be old acquaintances.

By all means change your pace to add drama to a chase or languor to a love scene, but that will come naturally if the story means anything to you at all. The more often you tell the more your confidence will grow and the easier the pacing will become.

Despite the similarity between the written and the spoken word there are profound differences for the listener as opposed to the reader. The reader

can absorb the tale at their own speed and look back at previous passages to remind themselves of the plot or who a character is. The listener is at the mercy of the teller as far as comprehension is concerned; it is for this reason that many tales contain repetitive sections or rhymes (e.g. 'So the second son went to the well, riddly tiddle tum, and met the old hag with a boil on her tongue'). These repetitions confirm the shape of the plot. Rushing though a story through nervousness on the teller's part will lose some listeners on the way. Pauses can be powerful and dramatic; they give an audience time to reflect upon what has gone before and to imagine what may happen next. Likewise, it is advisable to reproduce conversations between no more than two characters at a time; you may be able to produce distinctive voices for a whole crowd of characters, but your audience will need to envisage these strangers in their heads.

Look around as you speak until you have looked directly at everyone in the group, even if they number dozens, hundreds or thousands. They will all consciously or unconsciously believe that once you have caught their eye you have picked them out especially as the one person in the crowd who will really appreciate this tale. You now have a group of individuals who each think of themselves as special, which of course they are. This is a 3,000-year-old Greek orators trick that works despite the fact that you know that it is being done to you. If you use spectacles, peer over the frames and make sure that your eyes are visible to the audience. Beware the lighting; although it may seem sensible to sit the audience with their backs to the brightly lit windows, remember that all they will see of your eyes will be a reflection of the windows in the spectacle lenses. Contact lenses are preferable for the 'eye to eye' connection. Note your own reaction to not being eyeballed as a member of a storytelling audience; I feel illogically excluded when this happens to me. Giles Abbot, an experienced and highly accomplished English storyteller who is virtually blind, still manages to give the impression that he is seeing the individual audience members who are, in reality, no more to him than a vague blur.

There are, however, exceptions to this advice. Eyeballing the audience in some cultures could have an unintended effect; for instance, maintaining eye contact with New Zealand Maoris could be interpreted as an insult, whereas some African audiences may be more comfortable listening with averted eyes. These cultural anomalies must be treated with caution and learned alongside the language and customs to avoid embarrassing situations. Perhaps one should attend a local storytelling event to gain a 'feel' for the social mores of the people.

Be conversational, not declamatory in your delivery when you begin. There are many very good tellers who employ dramatic speech and well-rehearsed gestures to communicate their tale, but their performance can be intimidating for non-tellers who will assume, correctly, that many hours of assiduous practice are required to achieve this level of proficiency. If you start just as you would with a description of a day's shopping, you can ease into a tale. Start with something familiar or everyday and move gently into the fantastical. The audience will fly with you.

Many, many moons ago when dogs danced, and cats could curtsey, in the vast Red Kingdom *everything* was red. Tomatoes were red, sunsets were crimson, the grass was the colour of rubies and both the King and the Queen were royal scarlet (although the Queen had tasteful touches of pink in her most tender places). The sky, the earth and all things were red.

Bring them down again. Storytelling can become an all-absorbing experience for many people, taking them to emotional highs or lows not reached since childhood. 'Ground' the audience with some commonplace remarks as, or straight after, you finish a tale. There is a phrase at the end of the Roma tale 'The Red Kingdom', when the thousand-year old hero has at last died, that describes a man finding the hero's horse and his treasure. I infer that this ending was added to help a Roma audience to relax; to leave a horse or a hoard of gold lying about unclaimed even

though they were imaginary could give them a sleepless night. It may seem a pity to break the spell cast by an absorbing tale, but they must be returned to the real world in good condition by you; it was you, after all, who transported them to this magical place.

In conclusion, I realise that storytelling may suit some people more than others and that I blithely assume that everyone will find it as easy as I do. For this I must apologise. Storytelling has been my occupation ever since I was diagnosed with multiple sclerosis way back in the 1980s and it is my 'Element', as Ken Robinson uses the word in his splendid book of the same name on finding your 'niche'.

How to remember a tale. There are many methods; one or two will probably suit you better than the others. Rewriting the story using only a few words, retelling the tale as soon as possible and making a flow diagram of the plot using cartoon drawings are all used by some of my storyteller friends. My usual method is to use a combination of crude storyboarding (matchstick figures) and a few significant words. I retell it as soon as possible, usually to my wife Janni, who will tolerantly forgive lapses of memory.

There is a solution to losing the thread of a story in the middle, as once happened to me one sunny Saturday in Christchurch, Dorset, when I was surprised by loud wedding bells from the nearby church; take a dramatic pause, look around the audience and ask them, 'What do you think happened next?' This will probably only work once in a session, however.

If a tale is sequential; one section leading on logically to the next, then a simple list will do. Here, for instance, is an English sequential story called 'Lazy Jack', first as a list:

'Lazy Jack': Coin; jug of milk; cheese; kitten; joint of meat; donkey; dumb rich girl.

You can see that the key elements could just as easily be drawings or **Clip Art illustrations** like the following; if you have a memory that works best with things visual and a computer with Internet access it could be worth the time to do this. Much, but not all, of the Clip Art is free for non-commercial use.

Now as a Talebone with the key words emboldened:

Boy would do nothing but sit behind the oven and eat nuts. His **Mother** sent him to the **farm** to work.

1st day: Sweep the yard, **broom** wrong way up but paid a **coin**. Loses coin. Mother says, 'Put pay in pocket.'

2nd day: **Milks cows**, paid with **jug of milk**, puts it in pocket, spills it. Mother says, '**Balance pay on your head**.'

3rd day: **Cheese making**, puts **cheese** on head, so hairy cheese. Mother says, '**Hold pay in your hands**.'

4th day: **Winnowing** grain amongst mice and rats, paid a farm **kitten** in hands. Kitten scratches him and runs away. Mother says, '**Tie pay onto string and bring it behind you.**'

5th day: Works in **butchery**, paid **leg of meat**, dragged behind on string, cats and dogs bite it, ruined. Mother says, '**Put pay over shoulder**.'

6th day: Works with **horses**, paid **donkey**, takes it home over his shoulder. Passes house where sad, **dumb girl** lives with rich father.

'**If anyone can make my daughter laugh, speak or smile, then they may have her hand in marriage and half my fortune**,' says rich father.

Dumb girl laughs at **Boy** and **donkey** so, of course, **Boy's** fortune is made.

[In my version the rich father marries the Boy's **Mother** and the girl marries the **donkey**.]

Now I will tell the story of 'Lazy Jack' in told form, as near as it will go from speech into print. Do not expect to hear the tale like this if we meet; it changes every time I tell it, altered by the audience responses. I have included some hints and tips for a simple but relevant conjuring trick and some indications of how to include the audience.

Many moons ago, when pigs could fly and cats could whistle, there was a very small hut just north of Richborough Castle in Kent. In this hut lived a woman with a huge belly. Why do you think she had a huge belly? [Ask the audience] No, she wasn't fat; in fact, she didn't have enough to eat most days. Yes, she was pregnant, she was expecting a baby.

Now, when babies are born there is usually, as you [indicating the female members of the audience] probably know, a particular sequence of noises. Panting and maybe cries of pain from the mother, then a 'pop' [finger inside cheek then pulled outwards]. I know you mothers will say that this all seems too brief and easy but this is only a story after all. Then what is the sound that follows this? [Get the audience to imitate newborn babies. They will usually be too tentative and quiet so ask any mothers present if the cries were loud enough. They will usually say 'no' so get them all to be noisy.] But Jack, when he was born, found crying too much trouble and gave only a gentle sigh, 'Hoo.'

As he grew so did his laziness. Every day he would spend sitting in the cinders behind the warm stove eating nuts. When his Mother asked him to fetch some water from the well he complained that he didn't know which way up a bucket should be and that he couldn't find the well. His Mother fetched the water. When, a few years later, she asked him to go to the market and buy some ribbons for her hair he said that he couldn't find the road, let alone the market. So, she had to go herself.

Eventually he was so big and he was eating so much that his Mother said, 'Jack, tomorrow morning you must put on your hat and walk to the farm. The farmer says that he will find you work to do and he will pay you by the day. You will bring your pay safely back home to me.'

So, Jack set off the next morning thinking to himself, 'I expect the farmer will ask me what I can do. I will say "I can't do anything" and the farmer will send me home to sit behind the fire and eat nuts.'

But when Jack reached the farmyard the farmer was standing there with a broom in his hand and a smile on his face. 'Good day to you, Jack. Now, may I introduce you to my farm animals? These feathery things with yellow legs and combs on their heads are called "chickens" and they all make a noise like this…' [gesture to a few of the audience to make clucking sounds. Even the most sophisticated people will usually join in.]

'Now next to them these woolly animals are called sheep and lambs and they make a noise like this…' [Gesture to the next batch of people to make baaing noises.]

'Not to be confused with these things with slit noses and curly tails. They are called pigs and they make a noise like this…' [A new batch of people grunt, squeal and oink.]

'Now these dear things with horns and udders [gesture towards a predominantly female group] are called cows and they make noises like this…'

'Not to be confused with similar sized hornless animals called horses that make noises like this…'

'Now as you can see they all look very different from each other at the front and they make quite distinctive noises but what comes out of the back end of each is all much the same… and that is what you're standing in now. Yes, it is brown, and it is smelly, and it is called manure. Now, this is called a broom. A long pole topped with a piece of wood holding a bunch of bristles. Your job today is to use this broom to sweep all this manure out of the yard and into the gutter of the street, where it will be sluiced away to the stream and down the river then on into the sea.'

He handed the broom to Jack. 'I'll be back at lunchtime to see how you're getting on.' The farmer left Jack to do the job.

Well, Jack pushed the broom about but not much of the manure moved. He tried kicking it but it stuck to his boot and he had to wipe it

off on a chicken. When the farmer returned he was surprised to see that nothing much had been done.

'I can't get this broom of yours to work,' said Jack.

'Show me what you're doing,' said the farmer.

Jack demonstrated his technique and the farmer spotted the problem immediately. 'You'll find the broom works better with the bristles at the bottom,' he explained.

With the broom up the right way Jack soon had the yard cleared and the farmer said, 'My lad, you have done a day's work and you shall have a day's pay. Here is a coin to take back to your Mother. With this she can buy meat or cheese at the market. How are you going to take it safely home?'

[Take a large shiny coin from your pocket and hold it horizontally between finger and thumb with your palm upwards.]

'I don't know how to take it home – I'm only a lad who's never worked before,' said Jack.

'You're a working man now, me boy. Just take it home to your Mother.' Jack took the coin.

[Perform the 'French Drop' (or 'Coin Palm Drop') with the coin. The 'taking' hand covers the coin and mimes taking it while the hidden coin falls into the palm of the holding hand which swiftly forms a fist with a pointing finger indicating the (apparently) coin-holding hand.]

Jack suddenly realised that he was, indeed, a working man. Here was a heavy coin that proved it. [Look at your cupped (but empty) hand.]

'Look chickens, look woolly sheep, I have been paid, I am a working man!'

[Angle your cupped hand so the 'chicken' and 'sheep' members of the audience can almost, but not quite, see the imaginary coin.]

'Look pigs, look cows and horses; me, a working man.'
[On the word 'me' slap your coin-holding hand to your chest just above the shirt or jacket breast pocket and allow the coin to slip in. You are now, in conjuring terms, 'clean'.]

He danced out of the farmyard showing the coin to the birds in the sky, to all the shopkeepers and to everyone in the street. He danced over the bridge above the river.

'Look ducks, working man.' [Wave with your 'empty' hand.]

'Hello swans, look, working man.' [Wave with 'coin' hand and watch the 'pay' fall into the river.]

The coin splashed into the stream and sank quickly to the muddy bottom 'Oh no,' thought Jack, 'now I have nothing to take home to my mother.' He went home very slowly, wondering what to do. When he got home his mother said, 'Hello Jack, what did you get paid?'

'Well,' he said, 'I swept the farmyard and the farmer paid me a coin which I showed to everybody and then I dropped it into the river. I LOST IT. Waaah.'

His mother said, 'Jack, Jack, Jack, Jack, **Jack!** *Next* time you get paid put it in your pocket!'

[Prime the audience to listen for the words 'His mother said...' so they can be ready to join you in saying Jack, Jack, Jack, Jack, **Jack!** ']

The next morning Jack set off for the farm with his mother's words echoing in his head, 'Put it in your pocket, put it in your pocket.' On this day the farmer put him into the milking shed where all you dear cows [indicate the 'cow' group] had to be milked into pails and the pails emptied into churns which were carted off to the dairy. At the end of the day the farmer told Jack that he had done a good day's work and that his pay would be a jug of fresh, creamy milk.

'How are you going to get it home, Jack?' asked the farmer.

'Don't worry about that, Mr Farmer. My Mother has told me just what to do,' explained Jack. He very carefully eased the jug into his trouser pocket without spilling a drop.

On the way home he was so happy that he skipped and he danced. The milk oozed through his pocket and dribbled down inside his trouser leg, down his hairy, sweaty leg, squished behind his knees, soaked into his socks and cleaned between his toes for the first time since Christmas.

When he got home his Mother said, 'Hello Jack, what did you get paid?'

'Well,' said Jack, 'I worked in the milking shed and was paid a jug of creamy milk.' He pulled the empty jug from his pocket. 'Here is the jug. If you give me a dish I will wring the milk out of my trousers and my socks and empty my boots.' The milk was grey, full of hairs, and sprinkled with toenails and scars.

His mother said, [wait for the audience] – 'Jack, Jack, Jack, Jack, **Jack!** Bleugh! We can't use that! *Next* time you get paid balance it on your head and walk home nicely – and no dancing.'

'Yes, Mother,' muttered Jack.

'Balance it on my head, walk home nicely – and *no* dancing,' thought Jack to himself the next day as he walked to the farm. When he arrived he was put in the dairy to mix, wrap and set soft cheeses, which he did reasonably well. At the end of the day the farmer told Jack that he had done a good day's work and that his pay would be a large round soft cheese.

'How are you going to get it home, Jack?' asked the farmer.

'Don't worry about that, my Mother has told me *just* what to do,' explained Jack. He very carefully placed the soft cheese on his head. But it was a warm day and as he walked down the road he could see a dollop of cheese sliding down past his cheek. He stuck out his tongue and sucked the cheese into his mouth and it was delicious. While he was doing this another lump fell down the side of his neck and into his shirt – so he trapped it in his armpit. [Raspberry noise?] The next fell down his front and was trapped in his belly-button. [Raspberry noise?] He decided to ignore the piece that slid down his back and into his trousers.

When he got home his Mother said, 'Hello Jack, what did you get paid?'

'Well,' said Jack, 'I worked in the dairy and was paid a big round soft cheese. There is some here,' he pulled a splodge from his hair and threw it onto the table.

'It's got hairs in it!' screeched his Mother.

Jack fished around in his armpit. 'And here.'

'It's got curly hairs in it!' his Mother wailed.

'And here.' He retrieved the morsel from his navel.

'It's got belly-button fluff in it!' howled his Mother.

'And here.' He felt around in his trousers.

'We won't want that!'

His Mother said, 'Jack. Jack, Jack, Jack, **Jack!** Bleugh! We can't use that! *Next time you get paid hold it in your hands.*'

'Hold it in my hands, hold it in my hands,' thought Jack to himself the next day as he walked to the farm. When he arrived, he was put in the great winnowing shed to sort the wheat from the chaff, which he did by throwing shovelfuls of wheat into the air so that the breeze from one door blew the lighter chaff out of the other. He did reasonably well, despite the rats and mice running around and over his feet. These nasty creatures are the reason why farmers often wear string around their trouser bottoms – you don't want one of these sharp-toothed animals running up one trouser leg and down the other, do you?

Now at the end of the day the farmer didn't know what to pay Jack with so he asked Jack a question.

'Do you have rats and mice eating your food at home, Jack?'

'Yes, we do,' admitted Jack, 'and very hard to catch they are as well.'

'So would you like a farm cat to catch them for you?'

'Yes please,' said Jack. But he had no idea that farm cats are so *very* different from domestic cats. Your home cat sits by the fire and washes her whiskers and purrs when stroked. The farm cat lives outside in the foul weather and has tatty fur and scars all over from fighting; he wears an eyepatch, he's a pickpocket, he spits and he swears, he smokes thin roll-ups and keeps marked cards in his back pocket.

So the farmer put on a pair of long, thick gloves right up to his elbows and caught a fierce little farm kitten. It scratched and bit the gloves as the farmer brought it to Jack.

'How are – you going to get it – home, Jack?' asked the struggling farmer.

'Don't worry about that, my Mother has told me just what to do,' explained Jack. He put out his cupped hands.

The farmer put the kitten into Jack's hands and Jack leaned forward and said, 'Hello, liddle puddy cat!' and the kitten spat, scratched him across the nose, stole his hat and ran far away.

Jack went home slowly, wondering how he would explain his lack of pay and hat to his Mother.

When he got home his Mother said, 'Hello Jack, what did you get paid?'

Jack made a sad face and told his Mother how he had done exactly what she had told him to and showed her the scratches on his nose. When he told her that the kitten had run away his Mother said, 'Jack, Jack, Jack, Jack, **Jack!** *Next* time you get paid tie it onto a piece of string and bring it along behind you!'

The string was in Jack's pocket as he walked to the farm the next morning. Now, this is all set many hundreds of years ago when people still ate animals; pigs became pork ribs, cows became beef, sheep became mutton chops, chickens were roasted and even the horses were eaten by some people. [Indicate the audience 'animals' as you say this.] Jack was put to work in the butchery on his arrival at the farm; he had to sharpen the knives, scrape clean the cutting blocks and put sawdust down on the floor. At the end of the day the farmer told Jack that he had done a good day's work and that his pay would be a leg of pork to roast for his Sunday dinner.

'How are you going to get it home, Jack?' asked the farmer.

'Don't worry about that, my Mother has told me just what to do,' explained Jack. He tied the string onto the joint of meat, laid it on the ground and dragged it along behind him saying, 'Follow me.'

All the farm cats and dogs supposed that this was a game and they chased after it, tearing at it with claws and teeth. Jack wasn't having this and he started to run, the meat bouncing along behind him covered in a bundle of animals. Through the town, across the ford and into the woods, into one side of a hedge and out of the other and over the ploughed field until at last he got home.

His Mother said, 'Hello Jack, what did you get paid?'

He pulled the string and was surprised to find that all that remained of the meat was a tiny fragment of bone.

His Mother said, 'Jack, Jack, Jack, Jack, **Jack!** *Next* time you get paid sling it over your shoulder to keep it safe!'

Jack remembered this the next morning when he returned to the farm. On this day he was to work with the horses; he had to get them out of bed, take off their striped pyjamas, clean their teeth, comb their hair, take off their horse slippers and put on their horse shoes. [I usually have to admit here that I'm a town lad and that I don't actually know much about horses.] At the end of the day the farmer said, 'Jack, you've done a good day's work but all I can pay you with is my old donkey. He's been with me now for near thirty years and his back has gone swayed so me feet drag on the ground but he may do to take your Mother to the market. Would you like him?'

'Yes, please,' said Jack.

'How are you going to get him home, Jack?' asked the farmer.

'Don't worry about that, my Mother has told me just what to do,' explained Jack. He grabbed the donkey by the head and with a tremendous heave got the animal onto his own back. The donkey was old and wise but nothing like this had ever happened to him before. He'd had people on his back before but never had he been on somebody else's back. His legs waved in the air and he hee-hawed loudly right into Jack's ear.

'Hush, me old dear, me Mum told me how to do this,' soothed Jack.

The chickens all clucked [audience participation], the lambs bleated [audience participation], the pigs grunted, the cows mooed and the horses whinnied. All the people came out of the shops and houses and cheered saying, 'Most people ride the donkey; it takes a fine man to let the donkey ride him!'

He staggered down the road and past the biggest house in the village. It had a shiny front door with a window on both sides and two more

upstairs. *Windows*, silly, not front doors. This was where the Squire lived with his beautiful daughter. Now the squire owned all the land for miles around and he was very rich. His daughter was a beautiful seventeen-year-old with blonde hair and blue eyes and would have been attracting suitors from miles around but for one thing – she never, ever spoke nor smiled. She would sit at the window doing her sewing in the sun.

[This could be a good moment to select a female member of the audience to sit next to you with a straight face and mime doing embroidery.]

And why did she neither speak nor laugh? When her father had told her how her mother had died giving birth to her she had gone into a state of permanent gloom. The chaps trying to woo her had done their best; telling jokes, singing songs, playing silly tricks and making stupid faces, but never once had she smiled. Her father had even put up a sign on the town noticeboard:

> Should any man cause my daughter to laugh, smile or speak he
> may have her hand in marriage and half my land and fortune.
> Signed
> The Squire.

But despite dozens of visits from young men there had been no smiles, no laughter and not a word spoken. She sat at the window overlooking the front garden with a glum face and idly doing her embroidery. But on this particular day she saw something very strange. Beyond the hedge were four donkey legs waving in the air. Then a donkey's head leaned over the hedge and brayed at her, 'HEE HAW'. This was followed by Jack's face saying, 'Nothing to worry about, me Mum told me how to do this!' [Check that your volunteer 'daughter' is keeping a straight face.]

Her mouth grew slightly wider. Something was bubbling up inside. Her lips formed a grin. Then there was a giggle, then another, until they ran together into a real laugh. Not only a real laugh but her very *first* laugh. On and on she guffawed with never an inward breath. At last she ran out of air and with a last wheeze she crashed to the floor.

The Squire heard this and rushed down the stairs. 'Oh, my darling daughter, what has happened? Are you all right?'

'Father, father,' she wheezed, 'listen – I can speak and smile and laugh.'

'And how has this happened, my sweetest sweet?'

'The donkey and Jack looked over the hedge and they were so funny I couldn't help but to laugh.'

The Squire leaned out of the window and called for Jack and the donkey to come into the house. The end of the tale is obvious; the rich Squire married Jack's poor old Mother and his daughter married the one who had made her laugh – she married the donkey.

Remember, this is just how I tell the tale. Depending on you, your tastes and inclinations, who your audiences are and their level of listening skills, how much time you have available and dozens of other variables, the story, based only on the Talebone, will change. I recommend that once you have told the story that you never re-read my version; it is just one of more than a thousand versions of this ancient tale.

This was one of the tales that I chose to tell to an excited group of street children in Goa, India. Most of them had been blinded, disfigured or crippled in order to increase their earnings as beggars. One small nine-year-old boy ('I can speak a little Russian, some French and German, a few Swedish phrases, much Urdu and lots of American!') translated my words, one sentence at a time, into three Indian dialects as I told and afterwards said that the other children had two questions for me. Firstly, Why did I, who had nice trainers and a smart watch, need the "food stealing trick"? They used the same conjuring move that I had used to make Jack's coin disappear to steal small items from food stalls. They mimed putting food back onto the stall whilst retaining it in their other hand. The second question was, 'Why have you told us the same tales that our mothers and our aunts told us when we were small?' They were slightly different, as if wearing local costumes, but they were recognisably still the same tales. I then realised that those Celtic stories that I had mentally labelled as 'European' had travelled with Celtic traders as they had migrated East and West along the old Silk Road, past Turkey and Afghanistan, through the Hindu Kush, along the northern rim of the Himalayas all the way to China, also branching North and South on the way, spreading and collecting stories in all directions. Knowing this it is not surprising to realise that our European Cinderella is also Indian, North American and Chinese.

We are all storytellers

Storytelling is natural to everyone, if only as an 'internal dialogue' *(e.g. 'Now, I came in, took off my jacket, opened the fridge and got the milk; I put the kettle on and then checked the answering machine so where is my flaming mobile phone?')*. On a personal level, I only became aware of my own 'mental script' when one summer's day I accidentally turned it off. Rather like being rudely awoken by the *absence* of the chiming of the church clock just outside my bedroom window, when it broke down one night, my interior 'conversation' was not at all evident until it disappeared.

References

Books

Baker, Augusta and Greene, Ellin, *Storytelling: Art and Technique*, New York: R.R. Bowker Co., 1977.
 This classic book provides information on well-known storytellers, the purpose and value of storytelling, selection, preparation, presentation, program planning, and publicity. There are useful suggestions on storytelling in special settings or for children with special needs. This is an excellent introduction to the art of storytelling for the beginner.

Branch Johnson, W., *Folktales of Brittany*, Methuen, 1927

Briggs, Katherine M. and Tongue, Ruth L., *Folktales of England*, University of Chicago Press, 1968

Brunvand, Jan Harold, *The Choking Doberman and other Urban Legends*, Penguin Books, 1987

Calvino, Italo, *Italian Folk Tales*, Penguin, 1982

Campbell, Joseph, *The Hero with a Thousand Faces*, Princeton University Press, 1949

Cooter, Robert B., *Adventures with Words*, Black, 1998

Daily, Sheila, *Tales as Tools: The Power of Story in the Classroom*, The National Storytelling Association, The National Storytelling Press, 1994

Erben, K.J., *Tales from Bohemia,* Macdonald & Co., 1987

Hyde, Lewis, *Trickster Makes the World*, Cannongate, 2008

Lipman, Doug, *Improve your Storytelling*, August House, 1999

Robinson, Ken, *The Element: How Finding your Passion Changes Everything*, Penguin, 2009

Rosen, Betty, *And None of It Was Nonsense*, Scholastic, 1988

Rosen, Betty, *Shapers & Polishers*, Collins Educational, 1991

Shah, Idries, *World Tales*, Allen Lane/Penguin Books, 1979

Wright, A., *Storytelling with Children*, Oxford University Press, 1995

Zable, M.K., *Storytelling, Myths, and Folk Tales: Strategies for Multicultural Inclusion and Preventing School Failure*, 32–34, 1991

Useful websites

http://education.jhu.edu/PD/newhorizons/lifelonglearning/early-childhood/learning-growing/

> This is an article from John Hopkins School of Education about storytelling in the classroom called Learning and Growing Through Stories by Michale Gabriel, a Seattle-based storyteller.

www.yale.edu/ynhti/curriculum/units/2008/2/08.02.01.x.html

> An extensive article from Yale-New Haven Teachers Institute entitled *Storytelling as a Strategy to Increase Oral Language Proficiency of Second Language Learners* by Katherine Massa.

www.storyarts.org/index.html

Visit this website by New Yorker Heather Forest for a wonderful collection of short world tales and much more.

http://iteslj.org/Techniques/Jianing-Storytelling.htm@yahoo.com.cn
Storytelling in the EFL-speaking classroom
Xu Jianing Suzhou Industrial Park Institute of Vocational Technology (Jiangsu Province, China)

A look at the Chinese perspective.

www.pitt.edu/~dash/folktexts.html

D.L. Ashman's comprehensive collection of world tales.

www.ronatales.com

Rona Leventhal's website.

All the better to hear you with: Tips, Theory and Proof for the Educational Benefits of Storytelling

CHIP COLQUHOUN

The Proof

In 2013, the UK embarked on a bilateral EU Lifelong Learning Programme with Turkey. These projects were essentially cultural exchanges – chances for teachers of different EU member states (or, in Turkey's case, member wannabes) to experience teaching in other countries. But they each had a theme, and the theme for this project was storytelling in the classroom.

One of the UK schools involved had worked with me and my organisation, Snail Tales, on several occasions. Their headteacher was a great advocate of our work, championing our selection as the expert adviser for this project; and, just as the project began, she retired.

So, at the first project meeting – including dignitaries, officials, and teachers from both countries – the *new* headteacher from that school surprised everyone by asking, 'What's the point? Why should I bother committing my school to this project?'

It was a good question. For a start, taking part in this project wouldn't be cheap – her school would need to organise supply cover when her teachers were in Turkey, devote valuable lesson time to entertaining visitors from Turkey, and contribute a fair amount of administrative effort. But more significant for *this* headteacher was the fact that, at that moment in time, there was no hard and fast evidence to say that storytelling was at all beneficial in the classroom.

I don't mean there was no evidence at all. The broad benefits of storytelling in education are documented in academic works such as *Brain/Mind Learning Principles in Action*, edited by Renate Nummela Caine and published in 2005, and a quick flick through the UK's National Strategies archive will find many a report from a school who took part in the Department for Education's 'Talk for Writing' programme. But these are almost entirely anecdotal studies – i.e. collections of feedback from teachers, pupils/students and occasionally parents saying how wonderful it was to work with a storyteller and/or storytelling. A couple of controlled studies had been done, specifically in the area of teaching *science* through storytelling – in 1984 by Metcalfe et al., and in 1998 by Bailey and Watson. But although these studies compared the impact of storytelling alongside the impact of *not* storytelling, and although they noted that those who learnt via storytelling tended to achieve slightly higher attainment, they had some difficulty ensuring that both experiment and control groups were matched – not surprising really, since they took place in typical high school settings where the average ability of students in a class is deliberately varied (theoretically so the teaching can match the level of the children).

This EU project, however, mainly involved primary schools (ages 4 to 11), and in this arena there were *no* scientific studies exploring the point, or otherwise, of using storytelling in the classroom.

Now by this point I'd been storytelling professionally for just over six years. In that time I'd regularly enjoyed hearing from teachers and parents how their children had grown in confidence, concentration and creativity after spending time with me – and after 'straight' storytelling performances (I'm sure you're rapidly developing the opinion, from this book, that there's no such thing as a *completely* straight storytelling performance) as well as workshops. Notice too how I put 'creativity' at the *end* of that sentence: teachers often remarked upon how their pupils improved in *non*-literacy subjects, such as maths and science, simply because (in the teacher's belief) they were better at communicating their thoughts and/ or having the confidence to ask questions when they weren't sure of the answers.

But this headteacher's comments really bothered me. How could I go around extolling the benefits of my profession without full scientific backing? How could I live with myself if I continued to do so, with the nagging doubt that a proper experiment might in fact prove the opposite? I considered there and then that it would be for the benefit of storytellers, teachers, and children worldwide if a proper study was made into the benefits of storytelling in education.

So, that same night, I designed one.

It was pretty simple – I'm a storyteller after all, not a scientist. But I knew that proper scientific experiments needed (a) a control group, (b) both groups to be as matched as possible, and (c) a plan that could be <u>scaleable</u> and repeatable – i.e. anyone anywhere could have a go at the experiment, even with larger groups.

So, I picked a topic on which I was fairly sure neither the teachers nor the children would know much if anything about – the Chinese Qixi Festival

– and selected nine facts. I then asked the headteacher to select a class in her school and ask that class' teacher to split her children into two groups of matched ability as far as possible. One of those groups was to be taught those facts by rote for 10-15 minutes (this was the control group) while the other group only heard a 10-15 minute story containing those facts.

Straight after the time period, both groups were sent out to break. Immediately upon their return, all children were given a test of nine questions under exam conditions.

So, dear reader, which group do you think performed better in that test?

It's probably obvious, from the fact that this is a book on storytelling written by storytellers, that the storytelling group scored higher. But here's a trickier question: how *much* higher? What do you think was the average difference between the experimental group and the control?

Before I reveal the answer (for those of you with eyes that can't help but skim down a couple of paragraphs for the answer), I do of course recognise that the remit of this experiment was quite small. Factual recall isn't the only potential benefit of storytelling in the classroom, and in my own experience it actually featured quite low on the list of what teachers felt to be important. Only around 20 per cent of the comments I receive are along the lines of, 'My children remember what you told them so well!' Around 30 per cent are more like, 'My children really got stuck into our topic since your visit.' And around 50 per cent are a variation of, 'I can't believe you could keep my children's attention for so long!'

But for the purposes of a hastily designed experiment, factual recall was the easiest thing to test. The average difference in scores was only 25 per cent – which doesn't sound like a great deal, but let's look closer.

The average score of the control group had been 5.8 out of 9 – so rote learning helped those children remember the majority of the facts. That 25 per cent difference, though, meant the experimental group had an average score of 8 out of 9 – they had remembered *nearly everything*.

What finally sold it to that headteacher, though, was the fact that the rote learners had been told to learn – that is, after all, what rote learning means:

trying to learn! But the experimental group had *only* been told a story – the teacher hadn't said, 'You need to remember this,' she'd only said, 'I'm going to tell you a story.'

So, the learning of the experimental group wasn't just *greater*, it was also *automatic*. We finally had proof that storytelling wasn't just a fun thing to do in the classroom – it could actually improve test scores.

Although the experiment above caused all those on the EU project to become advocates for storytelling in education, we weren't able to progress the study further – chiefly because the political situation in Turkey would eventually cause the project to implode somewhat. However, we at Snail Tales have continued to press for this research. In 2016, representatives of both the Department for Education (DfE) and the Education Select Committee – including a government minister – came to visit one of our research schools, leading to a mention of our research on the DfE website, and key government officials now in our address book awaiting the conclusion of our research once it's reached. And then, towards the end of that same year, a researcher from the University of Cambridge joined the project, lending extra weight to its ultimate validity and credibility.

The experiments are still being refined, trialled again and again, and pored over to determine whether storytelling really can make a difference to children's *overall* attainment – i.e. not just literacy. So far, our results have been inconclusive – partly because we've encountered struggles similar to those met by Metcalfe, Bailey and Watson (trying to ensure both experiment and control groups have matched abilities, whilst also keeping the study randomised, scaleable, reproducible, etc.), and partly because, well, few schools and/or teachers want to be the control group! Most teachers seem to intrinsically accept that storytelling will benefit their children, so they naturally don't fancy their children being in the group from which it is necessarilyy withheld.

However, our data has at least shown that there are no *disadvantages* to having storytelling in place of 'normal' teaching (NB: what currently passes for the norm in the UK typically involves telling children their 'learning objective', explaining a principle to them, then getting them to practice several times until they can score highly when tested on the objective – in other words, learning by rote). In fact, our Cambridge researcher recently completed her own study into the use of storytelling in Year 7 (ages 11–12) science classes, and discovered that 'there appears to be a significant difference between the attainment of the control group and that of the experimental group. [...] a tentative conclusion can be made that using storytelling in science to teach conceptual understanding *does* improve students' attainment in those areas.' (Graham, 2018. NB: at the time of writing, Graham has not yet selected a journal to publish her research.)

But before I share with you my tips for using storytelling in classrooms, it will be useful to have an understanding as to *why* storytelling might be beneficial.

The Theory

Around 30,000 years ago, there were various types of caveman. The most famous are the *Homo neanderthalensis* (usually just called 'Neanderthals') and *Homo sapiens* (usually just called 'human beings'). In many ways, these cavemen were exactly the same: they wore clothes, made tools, went out to hunt, cooked their kill on fires, and spent their evenings decorating their caves with hands covered in pigments (e.g. ash from their fires). There was only one real difference: *Homo sapiens* began telling stories.

Whether they did this orally or not, we may never know for sure. But we do know that they used their hand art to create likenesses of themselves and other animals – almost like a comic strip of their hunting routines – while Neanderthal hand art just looked like, well, hands. *Homo sapiens'* exact reasons for capturing likenesses in this way is also lost to us, but likely suggestions include reminiscing on past hunts and/or planning future ones.

Either way, *Homo sapiens* were starting to develop *imagination* – the vehicle which powers memory, prediction, and a whole host of other uniquely human facets.

Most creatures, including Neanderthals, live (or lived) in the now – they may develop habits and behaviours over time as they notice that particular actions have particular causes, but in the main they're not prone to reminiscing about their day or planning the next week's shopping. In other words, they're opportunistic, relying on the current information entering their senses to make on-the-spot decisions.

Imagination changes all that. It allows us to call up past events and replay them in our minds. It allows us to conjure possible scenarios that haven't happened yet. It therefore powers ambition, hypothesising, and problem solving. It also enables empathy (the ability to imagine yourself in someone else's shoes) as well as behavioural analysis (strongly considering why someone does what they do) – factors that inspire altruism and Machiavellianism respectively.

In brief, though, the imagination allows us to *adapt*. And so, when the environment began to change some 30,000 years ago, *Homo sapiens* were able to plan a survival strategy. The Neanderthals were not so lucky, and are thus now extinct.

Which means, if you think about it, that storytelling is the most important thing human beings have *ever* invented.

It sensibly follows on, then, that strengthening one's imagination enables you to function as a better *Homo sapien*. So many of the subjects we encourage pupils and students to learn have, at their heart, the imagination. Numbers don't exist in nature, for example – we make them up, then play with them. Steam doesn't naturally produce electricity – we observe what nature does, and play around with putting different elements next to each other. Databases don't exist in nature – we invent ever-greater methods for gathering and sharing our knowledge. All of these ultimately led to inventions such as printing presses, the Internet, and smartphones.

I began sharing the above theory with participants in my storytelling workshops around 2008, and had the spiel above pretty well formed by the time I wrote it up for the EU's guidance on storytelling in the classroom that was eventually published at the end of our project in 2015. I then grew even more confident in this theory as it almost instantly became a *Sunday Times* number one bestseller that same year.

Though not one written by me. Dr Yuval Harari's book *Sapiens* goes into much more detail about the genesis of human beings than I (a storyteller, not an academic) could ever hope to do, but he too places the imagination as the keystone in the development of our modern intellect – or rather the bedrock of the global dominance of our species.

I'm sure storytellers worldwide will join me in sending Dr Harari our deepest gratitude. By lending his academic, well-researched support to a theory that we storytellers had already been made aware of by the joys and benefits of our daily practice, Dr Harari actually doubly confirms the principle. If we're reaching the same conclusion from two completely different starting points, using completely different methodologies, this lends more credence to the conclusion. And, as an academic, Dr Harari is able to spread the good – nay, essential – news about the importance of the imagination far wider than we storytellers ever could.

Even so, it just makes sense doesn't it? In 2013, the UCL's Institute of Education published a paper ('Social inequalities in cognitive scores at age 16: The role of reading', by Sullivan and Brown) which highlighted that children with a love of reading outperformed their peers *across the curriculum.* This paper effectively confirmed the link between indulging in imaginative exercise, and prowess in areas such as numeracy and science.

So, how can we improve our imaginations, and the imaginations of those we teach, to increase the brainpower, the attainment, and quite possibly the aptitude for life of everyone living in the world today?

The answer might just be in the book you're reading right now.

The Tips

As Tony Cooper mentions elsewhere in this book, the best way to practice storytelling is to tell more stories. That's because you will become more adept at employing the other tips he shares with you, such as remembering the 'Talebones' of stories (a trick I make use of, too), relaxing before you start, and looking at your audience.

Similarly, the best way to see the benefits of storytelling in the classroom is to tell more stories in the classroom! Like any other muscle, the imagination grows stronger with use – and the way storytelling engages the imagination is automatic, like a dusty loft in October.

OK, not *exactly* like a dusty loft in October – that was a terrible pun – but I'd bet a month's salary that you have an idea of what a dusty loft looks like. It doesn't actually exist, of course – it's only a simile. But you're able to have an idea of what it looks like because the words prompted your imagination to conceptualise it. Perhaps you pictured it. Perhaps you sensed it. How people experience the products of their imaginations is a personal thing. But the point is that just hearing the words of a story is enough to kick-start your imagination into *creating* the story.

It's for this reason that storytelling is unlike the majority of other artforms. It's not like painting, where the artist slaps their picture up on a wall for others to see. Neither is it like acting, where the actors perform their piece and then bow to audience applause. As a storyteller, you're more like the conductor of an orchestra – and every imagination in your audience is an instrument in that orchestra.

Essentially, then, your *audience* create the story – not you! You may have researched it, remembered it, rehearsed it even – maybe even improvised it off the cuff. But all the characters, settings and motion is ultimately crafted in the mind's eye of each listener.

You may already have spotted the secondary benefit to this automatic conceptualising. My term for this process is Imaginative Investment. When you invest in something – be it money in a house, time in a relationship, etc. – you care for your investment, right? The same is true with the imagination. As your audience create their own motion picture of your story in their heads, they are investing in it, taking ownership over it – and this leads them to care about the tale.

That's the reason why a story can be the best introduction for a class topic, raising the motivation of pupils/students to focus on the subject matter. Try it and see: make time to tell a traditional tale to your class, at least once a week, and see how keen your pupils/students are to discuss the characters' actions at the end. After just a couple of tales you'll find it easy to transfer that energy into exploring a period of history, an area of geography, the discoveries of a scientist, etc. All you need is a story to suit the subject – and here is where the Internet is the world's gift to storytellers.

What about encouraging your class to tell stories? It's true that not every pupil/student will want to jump up and tell a story, even if it's well-known to them or created by them – but that's most likely because they aren't confident in the reception of their ideas. Fortunately, storytelling also provides an easy route to building that confidence: Bigging It Up.

This principle is actually based on how we naturally develop language: we encounter something, and then someone tells us the label we should use to describe it (and possibly also the reaction we should have to it). Essentially this is another way of saying that the more storytelling you provide your class, the more you will enable *their* storytelling.

But the best way to do this whilst simultaneously building their confidence is to make use of *their* ideas yourself. For example, give your class the task of creating a story – you may choose to add in some set restrictions (for example period, place, genre), but the only essential requirement is that their stories contain some *drama*: i.e. something has to go wrong for their characters, and then the characters put it right.

Whatever results your class produce – and I can't stress enough my use of the word *whatever* – take one or two of their stories at random and have a go at telling them. But don't use their words – use your own. Treat their creation like a <u>Talebone</u> (again, see Tony Cooper's chapter in this book for more detail on this), and use all the storytelling techniques at your disposal to make it a story worth telling: a compelling opening, character voices, audience participation, etc.

Not only does this exercise gain you the Imaginative Investment of everyone present in the room (simply by virtue of it being an exercise in storytelling), but you gain even greater investment from the creators of the story – who will see the potential for their ideas to entertain others.

The more you do this, the sooner you'll find your class picking up on your language and/or storytelling techniques – meaning they too will begin their tales with compelling openings, carefully crafted character voices, considered moments for audience participation, etc.

All of which is fantastic for enhancing general literacy and/or enthusiasm for a subject – but what about using storytelling to teach a particular principle of grammar, such as the use of punctuation in writing? Or a mathematical principle, such as the decimal place?

These have been the main challenges in the research we've been conducting at Snail Tales – because they're also the main areas where children (and their schools) are assessed.

I should present a disclaimer here that our solution can still only honestly be considered experimental – not enough data has yet been gathered to confirm its effectiveness. But, as previously mentioned, no data has discredited it either. And with the observations from Dr Harari, the Institute of Education, and others – including the teachers who took part in the experiment below – I hope you will feel confident in giving this method a try in *your* classroom.

Again, our solution is simple, and probably not completely original – I'd be very surprised if I was the first storyteller to have tried something like this, and/or that no teacher had ever attempted it. In essence, the idea is this: instead of leading with the *learning objective*, lead with the *story*.

In practice, this means beginning a lesson with the *opening* of a tale. Take the character up to crisis point – the moment s/he realises they need to do something they've never done before, and/or something they believe to be difficult/impossible, to solve a problem – and then involve your class in the character's consideration of the problem.

Next, set your class the task of *assisting* the character with the problem. This should be done in real-time – don't say, 'We're going to just stop here a moment' or 'If you want to know how it ends, first we're going to have to do this'. Just seamlessly move into the task.

After the class have worked on the problem, let them return to their 'audience positions' (usually sitting in rows in front of you) to feedback their solutions, and try working them into the story using the Bigging It Up method. Use this to then end the story – perhaps completely, perhaps on a 'to be continued...'

I created a Key Stage 2 (ages 7–11) lesson plan along these lines for some of the teachers on our research project, giving myself the extra challenge of needing to find a story that the majority of the teachers would know. I used dice to select a topic at random from the syllabus as presented by the BBC's online lesson plans (which also helped me understand what a lesson plan looks like – I've always been a storyteller, never a teacher, so until that point I'd had no idea), and the topic was to be punctuation.

As a writer, I've always understood that punctuation is chiefly about how to reproduce spoken tone in written form. Thus, I felt I needed a story where the correct pronunciation of a sentence was key. This almost immediately summoned 'Ali Baba and the Forty Thieves' to mind. Although the passphrase in the story is the simple 'Open sesame!', I added the importance of *how* the passphrase was said to provide access to the cave. So, when Ali told his brother Cassim how to access the cave, and Cassim went and said 'Open sesame' (i.e. not as an exclamation), it wouldn't open.

The above became the opening of the lesson, and was immediately followed by a discussion between Ali and Cassim as to how they were going to write down the words in a way which would help them remember how to *speak* the words – a discussion that the pupils were invited to participate in. I then extended the story somewhat – instead of Cassim being slaughtered by the thieves on his first visit, he remains alive long enough to hear the chief thief change the passphrase ('Open sesame?') and has to record this for Ali.

The pupils were then set group work – listening to various passphrases from either the teacher or a teaching assistant, and working out the best punctuation to use. After 10 minutes or so, the pupils fed back to each other – first with the teacher reading out the efforts of the higher ability pupils, and then the higher ability pupils reading aloud the efforts of the lower ability pupils (that's another example of Bigging It Up in action, giving everyone the chance to meet at the same level). The story then concluded with Ali and Cassim eventually bleeding the thieves dry thanks to the pupils' help – though there was enough of the original traditional tale left untold should the teacher fancy using it to craft a subsequent lesson.

I did a similar thing with the numeracy topic of decimal places, this time with the story of Hercules' descent into the Underworld to fetch Cerberus. After telling the beginning of this tale, Hercules visited the Eleusinian mystics to learn the correct path into the Ancient Greek equivalent of Hell, and was told he had to follow a path signposted by descending decimal numbers. This lesson plan then followed the same sort of pattern as set out above: the pupils discussed what the Eleusinians meant, worked in groups to find the right path from a worksheet containing the numbers, fed back to the teacher, and received the 'reward' of the end of the story.

In practice, the teachers found that they had greater class engagement using this 'story-led learning' than they had ever achieved by telling their classes, at the outset, what they should be prepared to learn. Even so, I noticed some concerned looks on a couple of teacher's faces. When I enquired as to why, I couldn't help but smile at their response:

With this lesson plan, we actually covered the learning in about 10 minutes. But our timetable for this term gives us two whole lessons to cover this subject. So, what are we going to do with the extra time?

Why, gee – tell more stories, perhaps?

In my decade as a professional storyteller in education, I've used techniques similar to the above with age groups from pre-school to college level. The worst feedback I've ever had was that the participants were 'merely' engaged by my storytelling. The best has been a sizeable, holistic improvement in the participants' academic achievements, in a relatively short period of time.

I hope this chapter (and in fact this book) helps you experience something of the same.

My Journey into Storytelling

PETE CASTLE

'Peter is good at drawing.'
'You've always got your nose in a book.'

These two statements from my primary school teachers and my Nan
respectively summed up my childhood and so the direction I took through
school – both my choice of school and exam subjects.

It was always assumed, without much consultation with me, that I would
go into some form of art as a career, although no one knew much about
what that entailed. The trouble was I wasn't that good and by the time I

got to sixth form I was beginning to realise it. I could draw, and I still can (I don't really understand people who can't) but I couldn't really paint, sculpt, pot or anything else to a very high standard.

Then one day my art teacher threw out a question, 'Have you ever thought about teaching?'

I hadn't, but I did, and finished up studying to become an art teacher at Bretton Hall College of Education near Wakefield. I did a lot of drawing and took painting as my main study but, more importantly, found folk music and shadow puppets, and threw myself into the interests and crazes of the Swinging Sixties.

Ashford, Kent to Wakefield, Yorkshire: schoolboy to student. Both huge journeys.

Back at school two of my most influential teachers had been those who took me for English. One was a little, old, eccentric man who would have been far happier in a 1930s public school novel. Just before we left he invited our little A-Level group round to his house, where we played croquet on the lawn and swam in his pool! He was a real 'Gent' but I got on well with him and he taught me a lot. The other was a much younger, more outrageous man who wore pink or yellow jackets and was very camp, although he was married with children. He made my life a misery and I dreaded his classes, but I will be eternally grateful to him for opening my eyes and mind and kicking me out of my comfort zone. Both teachers hectored me for being too quiet, not joining in, not speaking enough, or writing enough! I would love to be able to invite them to a gig or to give them one of the several books I've written! They would not believe the journey!

After college I pretended to be a teacher for a few years but, to be a good teacher, education and the children have got to be your only interest. Your whole life has got to be dedicated to it. Mine wasn't. I enjoyed teaching the subjects I was interested in: we did a lot of painting, I produced some good plays, I got everyone singing and dancing and writing poetry. I couldn't be bothered with weekly spelling tests, or marking the register and collecting dinner money, although those things had to be done. I don't think I harmed anyone and I hope I inspired a few – that's all you can do.

Throughout that time, I had been building a reputation around the folk clubs, working semi-pro, doing gigs after school if they weren't too far away and more distant ones in the holidays. I also ran a couple of folk clubs and through that came across a group called Magic Lantern, who used shadow puppets. I booked them and struck up a friendship with them – especially their 'leader' Taffy Thomas.

In 1978, after all those little trips up and down the country, I launched myself onto the big journey, the one I am still travelling. I took the plunge and gave up my teaching job to go on the road full time as a 'folk singer' doing the folk club circuit and the occasional festival. I thought that, if I could do it for a few years, it would give me the chance to decide what else I could do for the rest of my life. I suppose there was also the idea of fulfilling the dream which I had had ever since I started playing guitar at about 15; I'd always written it off as just a dream, but could I really make my living playing music? Did fame and fortune beckon? No, to the latter. If I'd wanted that I wouldn't have gone in for folk music and definitely not the traditional English folk music which I specialise in!

In the mid-1980s, after a few quite successful years, I became aware of something which was happening elsewhere, completely unconnected to the folk scene, but which sounded similar: storytelling. What was it? How did it work? Who did it and where? I made a point of going to see a storyteller to find out what it was all about and, serendipitously, it was Hugh Lupton doing a set of English folk tales. I enjoyed it. My immediate reaction was – they're just like my songs but without the tunes. I wondered whether I could do it and worked up a couple of tales to use in schools. (I'd been doing quite a bit of work in schools since a head teacher, who also happened to be a folk club organiser, invited me in to sing to the school the day after a folk club gig. I enjoyed doing it, decided that I probably taught them more as a singer than I had as a teacher, and found that it supplemented the very meagre club fees very nicely.) My stories went well in schools, so I wondered whether I could put the odd story into my folk club set... that went well too and I have done the two in tandem ever since. That was by no means the end of my journey, it wasn't even a fork in the road, it was more of arriving on a dual carriageway where I could do two things rather than one!

By the time we moved to Derbyshire in 1987 I was billing myself as 'folk singer and storyteller' and doing a pretty equal amount of both. Then, and now, I am quite happy to limit myself to doing only songs or only stories if requested but, if it's up to me, I'll do a pretty equal split of the two. I find they work well together. You listen to a song in a different way to a story and it makes it very easy to make a balanced programme of light and dark. That was the road I travelled throughout the 1990s.

It was a very busy period for me and storytellers were in demand everywhere. Storytelling, as an art form, seemed to be accepted by arts organisations and funders in a way that folk music never was. There were grants all over the place from all kinds of people including, of course, the National Lottery. I was very busy telling in schools and libraries, at storytelling, arts and literature festivals, for the National Trust, at village fêtes, to all kinds of community groups ... and in exotic venues like ruins, caves, forests and on story walks – a form I very much enjoy.

I could have given up music and become just a storyteller, but I didn't want to do that so my new strapline, pinched from a review of one of my CDs, became 'a storyteller who sings half his stories'.

At that time, it looked as though we were heading for a boom in storytelling clubs. Some very successful ones sprang up in various parts of the country and tellers visited from other areas. Some of the clubs did swaps where the residents would visit each other and act as guest tellers. It looked as though a circuit of clubs, analogous to the folk club circuit, would develop and tellers would be able to learn their trade and gain experience by doing semi-pro work in them before they became professional. Sadly, that didn't happen. I was involved with running a couple of the very earliest clubs in Long Eaton and Derby, and we gradually learned that a storytelling evening does not easily fit the folk club formula because stories are, or can be, longer and need a slower approach. Very few clubs managed to consistently attract a large enough audience to book regular guest tellers and those that did were usually reliant on grants or Lottery funding. When the funding went, so did the club.

Sadly, I think, the storytellers themselves were partly responsible: they were often unwilling to adjust their fees to suit the amount of money available. The Arts Council recommended fee was £250, so they were going to charge that even if it was their first ever paid gig and there were only twenty people in the audience! Apart from a few larger, successful clubs, most storytelling events therefore became a small circle of six or ten enthusiasts meeting once a month and just telling to each other. Rather than meeting in pubs they tended to inhabit cafés; rather than beer and pork scratchings it was coffee and cake! There is nothing wrong with the pictures that either of those descriptions paint, but you can draw inferences.

As the years passed the idea of a guest teller simply telling a selection of stories started to be seen as not enough – the performance had to have a theme, the stories had to be planned through and linked together, a solo teller was not enough – s/he had to have props and a set and backing musicians. Now, a lot of the most highly thought of 'storytelling' is actually small-scale theatre. It's good, but it's not what we set out to do thirty years ago. Somewhere we have missed an opportunity. We could have had both, but we have somehow mislaid the grass roots.

I have no interest in telling any of the big epics. I don't want to do any stories, or sets of stories, which take a whole hour to tell. Most of mine are quite short – 5 or 10 minutes – very much the same as a song. In a way my stories work like the between song chat which many of the folk entertainers did back in the 1970s and '80s, people like Jasper Carrot or Mike Harding. Singers in folk clubs have always told jokes, shared little anecdotes about incidents which happened last time they sang this song and the like... which makes it even more amazing that some folkies are terrified of the idea of storytelling! For some reason they assume that it is going to be intellectual and arty and that they won't like it. On one occasion I was grudgingly granted a booking at quite a prestigious club on the condition that I didn't tell any stories! I found it very limiting because I was scared to introduce a song in case they might think it was a story! And it works the other way, too. Some storytelling clubs do not like songs although background music seems to be acceptable.

The next big step on my storytelling journey came in 1999 when I took over as editor of *Facts & Fiction* storytelling magazine. It had started in 1991 and since 1993 had been produced by Richard 'Mogsy' Walker, a very well-loved storyteller. I had contributed the occasional article or review so, when Richard announced that he wanted to pass it on, I offered. I wanted to ensure that it continued; I am big-headed enough to think that I could do it well, and I didn't want it to become the mouthpiece of any group or clique. I wanted it to stay 'independent'. After nearly two decades I still love doing it, although it can be infuriating and is a hugely time-consuming process. I've built it up so that it has more than twice the number of pages it had before and a lot more readers, although it is always a battle to keep the numbers stable. It is probably the only independent storytelling magazine in the world (i.e. not the newsletter of some national society) and that status gives us the opportunity to be a bit dangerous. We don't have to toe any political line or even be Politically Correct. *Facts & Fiction* includes anything and everything which can be classed as 'storytelling' and has a whole variety of approaches, from the silly to the studious, depending on the person who submits the article.

Some years ago, I decided that I would take it through to issue number 100 and then call it a day, but we are past that now and I already have subscribers up to number 109 so I'll be on that road for some time yet.

As the years pass the basis of my work stays pretty much the same; I'm still doing a mixture of songs and stories in a wide variety of venues. I've got to the age where I could just retire but I don't want to – if I go too long without a trip along that road to either a storytelling gig or a folk song club I get withdrawal symptoms. While I can continue to do it I will.

Where and when my journey will end I can't guess. With any luck it will be at the end of a performance with applause ringing in my ears! I hope I leave behind something worthwhile, whether it is a few of the stories which I've made, and which have been taken up by other tellers, or some of my CDs or books which, I hope, will continue to be read or listened to for decades to come.

Honest Liars: A Challenge for Our Times

MICHAEL WILSON

We are told that we are now living in the 'post-truth' age, a time when experts are dismissed as irrelevant and out-of-date, and carefully garnered evidence, painstaking fact-checking and calm, rational argument are written-off as elitist conspiracies, in favour of populist bluster, scapegoating and narcissistic posturing. We are in the age of 'alternative facts'. In early 2017 the *Oxford English Dictionary* named 'post-truth' its Word of the Year for 2016, with particular peaks in the term's usage around the time of the June

2016 referendum in the UK on membership of the European Union, and then again in November 2016 on the occasion of Donald Trump's election as the forty-fifth President of the United States.

I suspect that I am not alone in the largely liberal storytelling and academic communities that I inhabit, in being rather uncomfortable with this current state of affairs. To my own mind (and here I will lay my political cards right on the table) these two events on separate sides of the Atlantic were two of the most politically calamitous events in Western democracies of recent times, whose full consequences are still to play out. 'Post-truth' has become the weapon of right-wing ideologues, who have created a level of public discourse where the more outrageous the lie and the more loudly it is proclaimed (and then re-proclaimed at every subsequent opportunity with increasing volume, irrespective of the mounting evidence against it) the more believable it becomes. The soothsayers (be they the media, the judiciary, the writers and artists, or the academy[1]) have become the saboteurs, the traitors and the enemies of the people.

On the one hand, we might expect storytellers to be relatively comfortable with the idea of 'alternative facts'. From my own position I have long argued that storytelling allows us a different way of knowing and understanding the world and of challenging the idea of a single objective reality. Storytelling allows us to understand reality as much as a social, historical and changeable construct and, therefore, embraces the idea that there may be multiple and conflicting truths. Storytelling is one way that we might challenge the previously unchallenged orthodoxies and show new possibilities. As our colleagues in the Social Sciences might say – storytelling allows us to navigate our way through the complexities and 'mess' of the world.

So, it will come as no surprise that these recent events on the world stage have given me pause for thought and an opportunity to think more carefully about the relationship between storytelling and truth and, indeed, storytelling and lying, and in so doing, to consider how the responsibilities of the storyteller may be changing within the context of the post-truth world. Is there a new challenge that now lies before the storyteller?

In June 2017 I gave a keynote presentation to the International Conference on Storytelling for Health in Swansea, Wales, in which I attempted to begin a conversation about where and how storytellers might position themselves in a 'post-truth' world and argued for storytellers to be their own fiercest critics and to differentiate between different kinds of truth and lies, between those who would seek to enlighten and those who would seek to conceal and confuse.

But perhaps the notion of lying itself needs to be nuanced somewhat. 'Storytelling' and 'Lying' have always been willing, if occasional, bedfellows. I think of the delight taken by both tellers and listeners in the expertly delivered tall tale, told with a flicker of a smile and a conspiratorial wink, hovering between outrageous lie and believable oddity, a world in which the truth is an elastic concept, there to be stretched until it snaps. And I think of the World's Biggest Liar Competition, held annually at The Bridge Inn, Santon Bridge in Cumbria. In common parlance we use phrases such as, 'That's just a story' to pour doubt upon the veracity of a statement. And I remember my mother calling any child who was prone to making things up as a 'romancer'.

The crucial thing here, I would argue, is the relationship between the teller and the listener. In the case of the tall tale or the outrageous lie the storyteller is not trying to deceive the listener – enough hints are given through non-verbal language and the manner of delivery to make it clear as to the outrageousness of the untruth, whilst at the same time repeating the claims of truth. Nobody is taken in except the most laughably gullible, and that is in any case not the point. It is playful rather than malicious. It is the *confident* trickster, not the *confidence* trickster. In this ludic performance the listener knows that the storyteller is telling a lie and the storyteller knows that the listener knows, but both choose to play along in this elaborate and collaborative performative game, admiring the storyteller's inventiveness, verbal virtuosity and artistry.

In fact, this kind of lying is a form of truth-telling in that it seeks to draw attention to its own lies and thereby expose the kind of deceptive lying, as practiced by those in power. In theatrical terms this is a kind of Brechtian lying that says, 'Look, now I'm lying; see how I'm doing it; call me out and call me a liar. And now you know how lying works, seek out the bigger liars and call them out too.' It is this duality of the storyteller separating him or herself from the story which enables what Brecht called *Gestus*, the ability of the performer to simultaneously say one thing convincingly (the lie) whilst at the same time demonstrating to the audience their own *attitude* towards what they have just said (calling out the lie). For Brecht this enabled the performer to adopt a critical and political stance to the story. This is storytelling, therefore, that teaches us to discriminate between truth and lies, between those who act in our interests and those who seek to exploit us. Furthermore, this is storytelling that parodies the deceptive liars and laughs in their face, saying, 'We see you for what you are. Don't think you have us fooled for one minute.'

Jack Zipes conjures up the folkloric image of the honest thief to describe the 'genuine' storytellers who plunder the commonwealth of story to reinvent tales for our communities in our time. I might suggest that we should also adopt the moniker of the 'honest liar' to describe the storyteller who lies playfully to expose the bigger lies of the deceivers and con-artists. It is no coincidence that the World's Biggest Liar Competition bars entry to politicians and lawyers on the grounds of their being too well practised in the art and having an unfair advantage over the rest of us. Perhaps it is now time to rise to that challenge.

Note

1   As I was putting the final touches to this brief essay, staunch Brexiteer and Government Whip Chris Heaton-Harris, MP for Daventry, was busy writing to university Vice-Chancellors sinisterly requesting the names of all academic staff who are teaching Brexit-related material to undergraduates, along with copies of the relevant syllabi.

From Pen to Tongue

DEB WINTER

My father would walk into the room and say, 'He was not born a horse, and yet he bears a burden like an ass,' and walk out again, leaving the eight-year-old me confused but intrigued. As well as misquoting Shakespeare at random, he would recite long narrative poems as bedtime stories, but, having a bad memory, he would leap across the poem like someone jumping stepping stones. Having painted a picture of the Lady of Shallot quietly weaving in her island tower, he bounded over to the line: 'The curse is come upon me,' cried the Lady of Shalott.

Besides teaching me the valuable life lesson that terrible curses can suddenly fall on you without reason, these puzzling narratives led me to invent my own storylines, to fill the gaps in the plot.

Still today I enjoy plaiting the enduring threads of folk tales with the strands of invention and irreverent humour; creating a backstory for the wicked stepmother; making my own Cinders a tediously religious girl given to sackcloth and ashes, provoking the irritation of her two sisters.

But I'm leaping forward. How was the storyteller made?

The weapons available to the awkward, ill-fitting child are the Book and the Pen: hence at an early age I was a paper addict – even now I still press my nose to a novel and inhale the comforting smell of print; and a virgin notebook holds as much promise to the writer as a line of coke to others. Aged eight I wrote Enid Blyton-imitation books, even binding the pages and adding an inevitably short bio to the back cover: 'Deborah lives at home with her mother, father, Shadow the dog and Tricksy the hamster. *The Black Rose* is her first novel for children.'

Fortunately, my school was not on an island and so the peer-to-peer brutality stopped short of *Lord of the Flies*, but it was still a fearful place for the outsider, despite being policed with equal violence by a black-robed man with a cane and a Master's degree in sarcasm. I stopped speaking entirely at this point and retreated into print. A child can weave her own invisibility cloak if it saves her life. Wrapped in this silent invisibility, I passed through school and two universities (studying Literature, naturally) without ever speaking once in a tutorial.

Some pursue their dreams with confidence and determination from an early age: marine biologist; engineer; artist. But the girl who used to practice Juliet's dying speech as an audition piece alone in her bedroom knew it was useless to apply to Drama School as that would mean *speaking aloud in front of someone else.*

But sometimes the river carries us to where we are meant to be, even if we ourselves are paddling against the current. It just takes a little longer.

After paddling up many different rivers for a decade I finally found my voice. Past terror makes me the perfect facilitator of 'Public Speaking for the

Terrified' courses which I led for third sector service-users, volunteers, staff and trustees. I began a campaign against 'Death by PowerPoint', certain that it was the people's *stories*, raw and real, that were the most powerful weapons of the disenfranchised. I became an Associate of Speakers Bank, whose mission was 'Giving a Voice to the Silent'. I worked with women who had not been allowed to speak; women who had been silenced. With all sorts of people who had been quashed and cowed, one way or another.

I watched nine brave women survivors of domestic abuse overcoming terror to tell their stories to a conference of 'professionals' and heard that wonderful silence afterwards: the silence of shocked people *thinking*. *Learning*.

So absorbed am I in the stories from the abyss, the stories of the abused and the ignored, the stories of the survivors, and in working to get them heard, that for a while I forget that there are other kinds of stories. Stories of dragons and ogres; wolves and witches; selkies and swan-maidens and women made of snow. Stories that enthral and entrance. But others are telling them, breathing life back into them, telling them in new voices and the Stories themselves are growing stronger every day.

There is a 'Storytelling Revival' going on all around me, but I have a bucket over my head with the stories of the silenced-ones bouncing off the inside and I can't hear a thing.

But the old Stories are calling, louder and louder.

'We have truth too! Tell US!'

More coquettish: 'We're fun! You'll like us!'

Reminding me: 'You *know* us… you used to love us…'

The winning argument: 'We have magic!'

So, the Stories bend my footsteps to a performance of 'Wayland the Smith', one of the 'Storytelling Sundays' in Bristol. Martin Maudsley is there, one man on a stage – no costume, no props, just an armoury of imagery in his head and the energy of his own conviction. And out flow the words, the magical words that make me believe utterly in the swan-maidens, and then the songs of the swan-women flutter into the air with the voice of otherworldly improviser Ailsa Mair Hughes and I am hooked.

'How do you learn to be a storyteller?' is a question many of us are asked. I've heard many people answer: 'We are all storytellers,' which is empowering but can disappoint beginners genuinely wanting practical tools. I pass on Martin's advice to me: 'Tell to as many different audiences as you can,' adding my own two penn'o'worth: 'Listen to as many different storytellers as you can.'

A storytelling/improv workshop and a stand-up comic help me with my attachment to the safety net of a 'script' (the writer's 'besetting sin'). I learn that 'telling from inside the story' is not only critical but also helps with fear. I'm not a storyteller standing in front of an audience: I'm in the forest and the wolf is far more frightening than the front row.

I tell sea-stories to children on Barafundle beach dressed as a mermaid; to wedding guests huddled on damp hay bales in a deluge; to (accidentally) a slightly drunk audience who are expecting a stand-up comic. Learning all the time. I find myself in festival tents inventing euphemisms for sex because small children have wandered in; at a science festival telling cosmologists how the world *really* began; in an aquarium where I am upstaged by an escapee octopus.

I start running storytelling workshops for beginners and learn from everyone who takes part. I enrol on selected storytelling workshops to work on weaknesses and to experiment. As each year passes the pre-telling terror reduces just a fraction but not so much that the performer's friend, adrenalin, is lost. I work hard: I believe in the maxim that it takes at least 10,000 hours to learn any craft. After two years I'm braving Bristol Storyfest with two stories I've always wanted to tell, and the amazing Ailsa becomes both the Singing under the Sea *and* Orpheus. Some people cry and hug us afterwards and we feel happy.

I'm still writing with a passion, but with the *told* stories you can watch the emotions of the story ripple across the face of the audience. You're all in it together, and that's the joy.

When I impulsively emigrate from the woods of North Somerset to the cliffs of West Wales, where I know no one, and no one knows me, I find that the storytelling community there is warm and generous. I find a home in

Tenby Storytelling Café where Phil Okwedy invites me to co-host: a loyal band of regulars expands to make room for me. I discover the hospitable spare room-or-sofa-exchange-system that is such a help to the nomadic struggling storyteller. And storytellers' houses are never dull. Never having met David Pitt before, I try not to be disconcerted by the forty horses' skulls decorated with ribbons in his living room. Later, he enlightens this migrant to Wales about the Mari Lwyd.

However lovely the storytelling community, it is a long way back from Swansea or Aberystwyth or even Tenby to the far end of West Wales on a rainy November night and I devised a cunning plot. What if I were to get a regular Storytelling Night going in Fishguard? Lure wonderful storytellers to within a stone's throw of my own front door? Build the 'storytelling audience' where I live? Grow new storytellers? I made the mistake of enthusiastically telling lots of other storytellers that I was going to do that very thing. I had committed myself verbally in public, like a rash man at the altar, and now I was going to have to keep my promise.

I was conscious that I was the 'new girl on the block' and I didn't want to tread on anyone else's toes, so I tried to hunt down as many people already storytelling in North Pembrokeshire as I could. I found some of the people who tell stories 'off the grid' in green communities tucked into folds of the Preseli Mountains; I found Christine Willison, author of *Pembrokeshire Folk Tales* and this very book, living just a cuckoo's-spit from my door. We swapped life stories over a very long coffee in Ffwrn and now I had a potential co-host for the embryonic Fishguard Storytelling should I be struck down by beri-beri or footrot. I was anxious to make sure the new venture embraced both the Welsh and English-speaking communities and Christine comes up with 'Straeon Gwaun' for our Welsh name. I was pleased to be invited to work with locally-grown Mary Medlicott, putting on 'Why Stories must be Told' for the West Wales Arts Centre. I learned to love Facebook after all, because it helped me find other creative people in a rural area where we are all spread out across the hills and valleys.

So how did I get Fishguard Storytelling off the ground?

Without any funding (the Beyond the Border grant funding that had helped launch Tenby and Swansea clubs was long exhausted), I approached David Pepper who runs the café-restaurant side of the West Wales Arts Centre about a pilot three months. He agreed to let me have the lovely ground-floor, fully accessible café for only a small venue charge. Despite starting in the dark winter month of January, our audience numbers for the first three months were an enthusiastic 17, 39, 24. I used questionnaires to gather evidence of audience satisfaction and support, thinking about future funding.

From September onwards, the Story Nights drew a core of regular repeat attenders. The keenest agreed to form a small committee to make it not my venture but a community project: we had someone from a theatre background; a dancer; a Welsh language teacher. Audience numbers grew, occasionally dinted by rugby matches or storms. At the beginning we relied on goodwill and door money to bring in a guest teller, but I was keen to bring in other nationally-popular tellers to further build our audience. A successful application for Society for Storytelling seed money meant we could use the wonderful Wales Night Out scheme to book first-class tellers plus musicians (North Pembs audiences are very music-loving so accompanying musicians are popular). Two tellers generously donated their fee back to support the club. The Society for Storytelling money also helped my and the committee's morale: we felt a national body had noticed our work and was supporting us. Words of encouragement from David Ambrose at Beyond the Border and an offer to publicise our events were also welcome. It's good to feel part of something bigger.

I've had feedback from locals that attracting over twenty or thirty people to events in Fishguard in winter is pretty exceptional – being new, I didn't know that, but it was encouraging to hear. People in other areas have been asking how this was achieved, hence being asked to write this article. All I can do is tell you what I did and hope it's helpful to others.

So, what worked?

I found the critical thing in this rural area is making friends and telling everyone you meet about your project. Someone only had to sit next to me

at a music event, or stand next to me in the queue at the Co-op to have their ear bent about how great the Story Nights were. I never went out without a handful of flyers. 'Every time I see you in you've got a poster in your hand.' It's friendship and personal connections and relentless networking (enjoyable but highly time-consuming) that bring people in. You have to join other things and go to other groups' events to meet new people and personally invite them along.

Over my first three years in West Wales I must have talked a lot (!) as my own Deb Winter storytelling mailing list of fifty turned into a Fishguard Storytelling/Straeon Gwaun list of 190. Slightly quirky emails with good images are needed to remind people of events and lure them along. Bold striking posters; alluring marketing. There is so much going on here culturally that you are in competition for audiences. I laugh hysterically when former Bristol friends ask if I don't find it quiet in the country! The biggest problem is not clashing with someone else's event.

I asked advice about where to put posters, learning about the 'critical lamp-posts' to be fly-posted; garage-shops, rural pub noticeboards. Invest in a laminator and staple gun. Taking posters round is not enough, you have to talk your way round, chat to everyone. It takes ages but pays off.

Welcoming new people is critical. Talking to every person who comes to the Story Nights, building a sense of belonging. Getting to know names, having a sociable interval and introducing people to others, so that those coming alone (the majority) can feel they are all part of Straeon Gwaun, not an anonymous audience. Finding out if we have embryonic storytellers and closet musicians just waiting to be asked to participate.

It's worth sharing that we *still* have a huge job to do explaining what 'storytelling' is to the wider community. Most people I meet locally still don't understand what I mean by the word storytelling, either assuming it's for children or that it is an open mic where people are reading their stories aloud. Posters therefore do not attract them to attend, until someone enlightens them or brings them to an event.

Floor-spotters are both found and grown. People only started to volunteer to tell when they'd seen others and been inspired and encouraged.

Lots of hand-holding, helping, and reassurance was needed. The host/ MC role is critical: you need to be nurturing and empowering. It can be a difficult balance between inclusivity and quality though if you are charging audiences, one that has to be negotiated with tact – and firmness about *time*: we've all experienced the rigor mortis that sets in when spoken word 'open mic' sessions drag on for hours. Part of the cunning plan was to run Storytelling Skills workshops and that has proved popular. We secured one of a small number of Gwanwyn Festival community grants from Age Cymru, with our project 'Spring into Storytelling' being embraced enthusiastically by the over fifties, sixties and seventies.

A handy tip passed on by our host venue was to go 'on tour' to other local venues in order to reach their regulars too – rather than being precious about Straeon Gwaun 'belonging' to them, they are keen for us to build partnerships. A meeting is planned with the local youth project and other arts groups. Recently I walked around the woods with a community development worker (I've started initiating walking-meetings as a way to spend more time in the woods) about bringing storytelling to a Festival of Death he'd like to organise to start conversations about dying well. A promising collaboration in the making. If he forgives me for dragging him through the deep mud of Pengelly Forest.

Anything else I've learnt? Be evangelical about storytelling. Carry flyers in your rucksack or handbag. Approach anyone wearing colourful ethnic or hand-knitted clothing or with Interesting Hair: they may be story-lovers, creative people or festival-goers! Approach people in sober clothing – *everyone* loves a story. Be friendly to strangers (apart from fake old crones offering you rosy apples). Give a flyer to the garage when you take your car in; the plumber when he calls; the art gallery owner; the till-assistant. Listen to advice on publicity from people who've lived there longer. Never speak ill of anyone. Try not to take sides. Speak well of people behind their backs. Be inclusive. Thank the committee and anyone who does anything for you, from low-cost printing (Theatre Gwaun) to the person taking a poster to distant yurt-dwellers. Provide cake at committee meetings. See everyone

you meet as a potential friend or at least a potential audience member or floor-spotter.

Getting Fishguard Storytelling/Straeon Gwaun going has taken a huge amount of voluntary time: mine and the committee's. But we are growing like a slowly-rolling snowball and more and more people you meet say, 'Oh, I've heard about the nights at Peppers…I must come along.' The rewards of storytelling and growing a local storytelling community? Meeting people who share your passion for words; falling in love with new stories; watching the faces of the listeners; seeing a new teller blossom into confidence; the fear and thrill of improvisation; spending more time in Annwn than in the upper world, watching people make friends; fighting bigotry by sharing stories and goodwill across races and cultures. Telling and hearing the Stories. We are all just catalysts who let the Stories come to life and work their magic.

So, come to Straeon Gwaun all you silver-tongued truth-tellers and larksome liars and let the Stories out!

Blooming Flowers and Stony Stares: Negotiating Identity through Story

EMILY UNDERWOOD-LEE

When we tell stories, we are showing the world something of ourselves and how we want to be seen. The stories we choose to tell or seek out in performance and in our personal lives speak to and about our current situation and preoccupations. Stories can also show us something of the world we wish to inhabit, or to quote Marina Warner, stories 'offer the possibility of change, far beyond the boundaries of their improbable plots or fantastically illustrated pages' (Warner, 1995, p.xii). It is my contention here that, by thinking of stories as an opportunity to construct our own representations of ourselves and the world, we can think of stories as a hopeful space.

Two memories…

Summer 2017

I sit with my nine-year-old daughter listening to Sally Pomme Clayton tell the story of Demeter and Persephone. We are lounging on cushions and rugs beneath fruit-filled apple trees, the summer sun is filtered through the leaves and we can see bumblebees moving around the packed flower beds. My daughter rests her head against me and I hold her hand as we listen to tales of Persephone's ribbon, lost and found, at the gateway to the Underworld, and of the goddess of fertility's search for her stolen child.

Autumn 1982

I am a child, I sit in my bedroom, surrounded by pink striped wallpaper, a clock in the shape of a giant wristwatch ticking away. My parents have recently taken me and my brother to a gallery. A painted shield decorated with a 'lady with snakes in her hair' stays with me. I beg my mother to tell me again the story of the great beauty punished by the jealous goddess and her ability to turn men to stone. I revelled in her rage. I was spellbound by the power of her beauty and the even greater power of her terrifying transformation.

Demeter and Medusa's stories are tales I have always loved. I was raised and nourished on these tales and many more. Although the two very different and uniquely womanly stories of Demeter and Medusa that I recall above have spoken to me throughout my life, my responses to them have differed as I have negotiated my way through various ages, roles and identities. Of course, it is not simply my situation that has changed the way I respond to stories and many things combine to make an audience member feel connected to a story (or not) including the skills of the teller, the setting, the company they are in and much more besides. Certainly, Sally Pomme Clayton is a skilled and charismatic teller, the secret garden filled with apple trees and flowers was an enchanting setting, and listening while my daughter snuggled into my side was idyllic; similarly, my mother was also a brilliant story teller, her enthusiasm and energy with a story would never fail to delight me, and the cosiness and safety of my childhood bedroom was conducive to attentive and satisfying listening. In this brief essay, however, it is my reaction to the *characters* and *narrative* of the story with which I am concerned. On these two remembered occasions I had responses to the stories that I had not had before, and I propose that it is my relationship to the *essence* of the story and how I was able to relate it to my own circumstances that changed. Demeter's story spoke to me as a middle-aged mother grappling with anxiety and fears about raising daughters, whereas as a young girl negotiating femininity and identity, I was drawn to the story of Medusa and her petrifying feminine powers and punishments.

Of course, I am reading my own interpretations into these stories and they may speak very differently to other listeners and tellers. I do not, for example, know what Pomme's motivation for choosing to tell this particular story was. However, whether explicitly or covertly, the stories we choose to tell will always reveal something about us and, if they are to 'work' for an audience, I believe that they will always enable listeners to discover something new about how they see, or would like to see, themselves. When I listened to Pomme telling the tale of Demeter in the Secret Garden at Tretower Court I was so moved because I was able to see possibilities for how I might understand my own position as a mother.

Beyond their function as a mirror that can reflect back to us and help us reflect upon our own identity, stories also serve to help us imagine ways in which that identity might be negotiated, changed and mediated. This thinking about who we are and who we might be through stories is a powerful and hopeful political act. By presenting stories we are making meaning and we are opening up possibilities. When we see ourselves and others in stories we are confirming or countering cultural stereotypes. By showing how this particular mother (Demeter) is represented we are saying something about all mothers and we are imaginatively creating a notion of what mothers *could be*. To take this further I turn to a rather eloquent argument about the power of the artistic imagination from Harvie and Weaver who state, 'If you can imagine something, you can make it, and if you can make it, you can change it' (Harvie and Weaver, 2015, p.13). Following Harvie and Weaver's argument, the first step to making a change is to imagine that the change is possible. When we see Demeter as a model of what we could be and when we tell her story through the lens of imagining other ways of mothering we are beginning to make that change possible.

Jack Zipes has often championed the imaginative possibility afforded by story and indeed counts this as one of the very reasons for making art in the first place. He states, 'It is our realisation of what is missing in our lives that impels us to create works of art that not only reveal insights into our struggles but also that shed light on alternatives and possibilities to restructure our mode of living and social relations' (Zipes, 2010). Here stories not only allow us to imagine other ways of existing but reveal the cultural conditions that have constrained our options for ways of being in the first place. Drawing together the arguments from Zipes and Harvie and Weaver we might suggest that stories not only allow us to show how we are culturally defined, but also to imagine a way of breaking away from that definition to a whole new realm of ways of being and understanding our identity within a changeable world.

Autumn 2017

I tell the story of Demeter and Persephone to both my daughters. We sit together at our kitchen table and we remember other times we have heard this story told. We talk about what it means to be a mother who will search through the world(s) to rescue her daughter and what it means to be a daughter who might want to be rescued. We open a pomegranate and squeeze the juice from the seeds.

By thinking about this story my daughters and I were able think about the social order that constructs mothers and daughters in certain ways and to align ourselves with or challenge these representations. We were able to find our own places within the story and to see a reflection of the world we currently inhabit. I was able to explore for myself the kind of mother I aspire to be and the kind of mother I want my children to think I might aspire to be. Demeter becomes metaphor for all I want to say and to have said about motherhood and for me to make the first small steps to mothering differently.

All these versions of both mother and daughter help us imagine a potential future, a world we don't currently inhabit but might like to. And as Weaver and Harvie state, the first step to making change is to imagine that change is possible.

References

Aston, E. and Harris, G., *Feminist Futures? Theatre, Performance, Theory*, Basingstoke: Palgrave Macmillan, 2007

Harvie, J. and Weaver, L., *The Only Way Home is Through the Show: Performance Works of Lois Weaver*, Bristol: Intellect, 2015

Smith, S., *Subjectivity, Identity, and the Body: Women's Autobiographical Practices in the Twentieth Century*, Bloomington: Indiana University Press, 2015

Warner, M., *From the Beast to the Blonde: On Fairy Tales and their Tellers*, London: Random House, 1995

Zipes, J. 'Utopian Tendencies of Oddly Modern Fairy Tales', *YouTube*. Available at www.youtube.com/watch?v=aMdLXij02fU (accessed 24 March 2015)

Still Sorting the Sock Drawer: The Ever-Changing Story of a Life-Changing Diagnosis

EIRWEN MALIN

Medron was a good king; kind, just and surprisingly progressive. The country prospered. But there was something wrong, something wrong with Medron himself and he knew it. It all started when he noticed that the sole of his right shoe kept wearing out much more quickly than the left.

After several years of occasional visits to the GP surgery with odd and unexplained symptoms, one of the GPs referred me to a neurologist 'to put my mind at rest'. After nearly twelve months of waiting, I finally got my appointment and the consultant unexpectedly, and with somewhat clumsy practice, diagnosed Parkinson's Disease (PD), a degenerative, incurable neurological condition which, according to him, is 'devastating in its later stages'. My world had been upended but the good(?) news was PD does not particularly shorten lifespan. You just have to learn to live with it, potentially for a long time.

I went back to the GP a few days later, wondering what happens next. I discovered that part of the answer was, get back in the queue, and wait again, to see a PD specialist. Of course, in those intervening days I had been busy Googling, I had some answers, lots more questions, and the need to rethink my priorities for the coming years. I wasn't ready to face work or work colleagues at that stage and the GP suggested two weeks' adjustment leave. What he actually said was, 'Go and sort the sock drawer,' and so the story of a story begins.

There was no diagnosis for Medron, of course. The point of change came for him one winter's day when he was sitting in his room looking out of the window at his beloved garden. Behind him and across the room a newly lit fire was spitting in the grate. A spark that flew out ignited the hearth rug, and though thick black acrid smoke began to fill the room and alerted the servants, Medron's loss of sense of smell made him vulnerable and he was nearly trapped by the fire. How could he look after the country when he couldn't even look after himself?

Even before I saw the specialist I learnt a lot about Parkinson's. I made simple changes to life that helped mitigate some of the varied and pesky symptoms. I had put some longer-term plans in place and had stopped calling it a disease and used the term condition. Life was returning to some sort of normality when I was struck by a thought: 'The best thing to do with a bad experience is to make use of it.' I'd been involved in stories and storytelling for more than twenty-five years and now it was time to tell my own story, and the idea of 'Sorting the Sock Drawer' began to unfold.

One of the frightening statistics I discovered about Parkinson's is that over 80 per cent of those with the condition have speech and/or communication difficulties. The thought that something might steal my voice, while I still had something to say, horrified and frightened me. I needed to get on with this while my voice could still be heard.

Medron was last at everything, last to finish his food, last to be ready for hunting, last to agree a decision at council and he sensed that everyone was losing patience.

From the outset I'd decide not to create a straightforward personal story but envisaged the stories of two protagonists intertwined, one a mythical character the other myself. I'd always had a love of, and a belief in, the special power contained within a tried and tested traditional story, a notion that the passage of years and many tellings distilled the truth or essence of a story. Story also plays a special role in allowing listeners to learn, understand and empathise without having to have a direct experience. I searched, with little success, for a traditional story to work with. I was a bit stuck, then a dollop of serendipity was dished up; I was reminded that Hans Christian Andersen himself created stories influenced by the traditional stories of Europe. If it was good enough for HCA it was good enough for me and I decided to create the mythical part myself.

I should point out at this point that the analysis below did not evolve in the coherent form that is set out. I was not actively conscious of all the elements, but my subconscious, highly influenced by story, was obviously hard at work and on reflection it was doing a good job.

Purpose

From the beginning I wanted to raise general awareness of the impact Parkinson's has on life. As I came to terms with having the condition and told friends and colleagues, it was soon very clear that few knew anything much about it beyond the tremor. When a generally well-informed friend said, 'It's just a matter of taking a few pills, isn't it?', I realised there was a job to do in helping people understand the impact of the many, varied and often invisible symptoms.

My contact with the Parkinson's community had made me realise that many of those with the condition were also unaware of some of the simple things they could do themselves to make life a little bit better. So, there were messages I wanted to pass on to them too. I wanted to help them know they could take control.

Medron and his most faithful advisor hatched a plot.

Fortunately for me, I had discovered some positive aspects of life with Parkinson's and I wanted to convey the message 'Life is different but not necessarily worse.'

Format

And so it was that less than two weeks later, with his people lining the streets to cheer him on, Medron set out on his quest.

The shape of the fictitious strand seemed obvious from the outset: people often refer to life with Parkinson's as a journey so the familiar story outline, home – away – home, was perfect. A protagonist has a problem and sets out on a journey to find answers, along the way they meet different people, have adventures and return home to a different life. Each encounter teaches the protagonist something about the world and something about themselves, and the new life they create for themselves on return forms the resolution of their original problem. My personal story would then be a separate strand juxtaposed with the fictitious, two stories running parallel.

Choosing a Protagonist

My first instinct was to choose a king, then I began to doubt. Should I have a female protagonist? I considered and decided that the subject matter was not particularly gendered, as some medical conditions would be, and as my story would give a female perspective. King Medron provided a character with whom male listeners might identify, with a higher percentage of men diagnosed with Parkinson's than women, a factor to consider.

Development of the Plot – An Ongoing Story

Long familiarity with myth and traditional story made the initial creation of Medron's story relatively straightforward. Fitting my story in between the segments so that Medron's understanding or achievement in each part was mirrored by my own story was an interesting process. As I considered the incidents from my instinctive plot and matched them to my actual experiences I found myself clarifying the expression of my own thoughts, feelings and reactions. Sometimes this process changed Medron's story.

> *Medron could see the boy was too ill to walk any further. 'I will come with you to the healers house,' he said. 'I will walk and the boy can ride my horse.' Medron was pleased to be able to help.*

Something unexpected was coming out of the process of developing a performance, it was helping me to understand and express my own reactions to my changed life. 'Sorting the Sock Drawer' has been performed a number of times in the last 18 months or so and both Medron's story and mine are changing in subtle ways each time, as my life, learning and priorities change. A new symptom or a new strategy for mitigating an existing one will creep in to the next performance.

And as the two of them talked long into the night, with arms waving as they enthusiastically gesticulated, their shaking hands were like a pair of dancing butterflies.

The more I considered the plot the more focussed became the messages I was trying to convey. The detail of the incidents exemplified the very specific learning from each adventure, and the overall environment in which the plot resides underscores deeper messages, such as who has power to act, who are the keepers of knowledge, how to prioritise what is right for your own life and where truth lies in a confusing world.

Medron remembered his quest and started to look in earnest from some task or challenge to achieve or a foe to conquer.

I now feel as though the plot lines are settled; however, I am only three and a half years in to what might be a twenty-five-year journey of decline, so who knows? All the time new research comes to light and I try to squeeze in useful information. I suspect it will have a long shelf life, but, if there is a sudden discovery of a cure, I won't mind a bit that 'Sorting the Sock Drawer' will be irrelevant.

Use of Humour

One wouldn't choose to develop Parkinson's but on the positive side, and there are some positives, it gives you entry to a new community of people. And what a community it seems to be, full of lovely, positive, welcoming people with a much higher than average sense of fun and wicked sense of self-deprecating humour. I have echoed that humour in the telling of my story particularly. In entertainment terms the humour releases the tension of potentially difficult listening; in terms of learning it helps people remember the message.

Performances

Away from the pressures of state, with unaccustomed exercise and a more rustic diet in the wayside inns, Medron began to feel healthier. He enjoyed his days of riding, the ready companionship he found each evening and the wonderful worry-free nights of sleep.

The piece has been performed to different types of audiences and been well received by all. Storytelling audiences have accepted it as straightforward performance. People with Parkinson's who have attended have made comments like 'It's the story of my life', have identified with the issues raised and also found it uplifting. Those who don't know about Parkinson's tell me they have learned a lot.

Some performances have been followed by a discussion, either straightforward reactions to the piece or to stimulate a particular type of discussion. It was part of a series of events for Dying Matters week and been part of a Storytelling in Health Conference. I used it myself as part of a study tour in the USA to stimulate discussion on where people get information on neurological conditions like Parkinson's.

Conclusion

Occasionally the Princess Ileri, now Queen, or some of the courtiers would seek out Medron to ask his advice on important matters. He was always happy to help, if they could find him. Quite often he was away, with Ildreth, having adventures.

I think the show as it has developed has fulfilled its aims

- To raise awareness of difficulties and issues
- To inform and empower life improvement
- To inspire and encourage positivity

Unexpectedly, it has also helped me to think things through. You should know, though, that I still have a drawer full of odd socks.

For further information visit: https://sortingthesockdrawer.wordpress.com/sorting-the-sock-drawer/

Acknowledgements

Many thanks to George Ewart Evans Centre for Storytelling at the University of South Wales and to Dr Emily Underwood-Lee for encouraging the development of the piece and for hosting the first performance.

Note

This telling took place at the Beyond the Border 'Tales from the Tall Tower' Festival at Tretower Court on Sunday, 27 August 2017.

Finding my Jewish Stories

LIZ BERG

My first residential storytelling weekend. I was scared. All the others seemed to have been telling stories for years and although I was older than most, I was very much a newbie. Xanthe Gresham was leading the weekend in Derbyshire. We all sat in the well of this old mill house on banks of soft-cushioned chairs. 'Well,' she said, 'someone tell me a story.'

The circle was blank, silent. Then I put my hand up and I told The Arrow. 'Thank you,' she said, 'I hadn't heard that framing story for it before.'

I was surprised. The framing story was so well known to me, it went together with *The Arrow*, as long as I've known them. It spoke of the Dubno Maggid, an itinerant Jewish charismatic preacher, who had been asked why his stories always hit the spot. He answered them with the story of The Arrow. They were the stories his listeners needed to hear at that time.

In an early beginner's workshop run by Graham Langley, I was paired up with this man and we were told to tell a story from the top of our heads. 'Oh,' I said, 'I will tell this Jewish one.' 'Stop right there,' he said. 'I don't want to hear anything religious.' In vain, I said it wasn't religious at all, it had a joke in it! He didn't want to know. So, I switched to a Welsh story. I never saw him again.

As my learning progressed through workshops, tellings in pubs, festivals, gardens and finally clubs, I found the stories I was drawn to tell the most. Jewish stories. Ashkenazi (East and Middle European) and Sephardi (Spanish and Portuguese) and later world Jewish stories.

As a child I had loved hearing/reading stories of Elijah the Prophet. He was so magical, appearing often as a rosy-cheeked old man, a beggar, to test people, to give presents to those worthy enough, to help people to endure their woes. I looked for as many stories as I could about him. I found some in the Talmud, the Oral Torah. I found others in Jewish books for children such as *The Kingdom of the Birds* and *The Adventures of K'tonton*. I lapped them up and, somehow, they remained in my memory.

When I was in shul, synagogue, and the rabbi was speaking, they would invariably have a story to tell. Not one found in the Bible, but perhaps one about the Hassidim. Those stuck in my head too. Not only are there books written on the tales of the Hassidim but one, Rabbi Nachman of Bratslav, wrote a book of Hassidic tales that cloaked mysticism in story. One of his is *The Rooster Prince*, where the son of the king thinks he is a rooster, takes off his clothes and pecks at his food on the floor without speaking except crowing. No one can cure him until a Jewish sage comes and sits naked with him under the table and gradually introduces him to speaking, clothes and eating off plates on the table until he is acting like the prince again. Other stories of his had princesses, mermaids and demons, my kind of story!

When I was teaching Judaism, I always told jokes, Jewish jokes. These got more and more detailed and soon I was telling stories. But where to find more? Someone bought me one of Howard Schwartz's compilations

and I was off. *Miriam's Tambourine* opened my eyes to Jewish stories from around the world. Peninnah Schram's *Stories within Stories* had stories I already knew but with framing stories round them. I gave a copy of her *Stories One Generation Tells Another* to my daughter, so we each had a copy. I scoured bookshops and found the *Encyclopaedia of Jewish Mysticism and Magic*, even a children's tale from Arnold Wesker (he signed a copy of one of his plays for me a year or so before he died). I went to English translations of Yiddish writers like Peretz, Shalom Aleichem, Yiddish folktales such as that compiled by Beatrice Silverman Weinreich, translated by Leonard Woolf, including parables by the Dubno Maggid. Sephardi stories came my way by accident, yet one of those tales I frequently tell is about a mermaid and a princess. I have a French Jewish story I bought on spec.

The crowning glory for me was on a trip to Israel. I knew that the University of Haifa held the Israel Folk Archive, started by Professor Dov Noy in the 1950s. There were kept verbatim records of stories told by immigrants from all over the diaspora, as well as indigenous Jews. They had started to translate the stories and sayings into English – a mammoth task.

On my visit, they gave me free rein to look through what they had published in English. They showed me how they were painstakingly transcribing the stories collected from the fragments of paper onto the computer, before they could be translated into any language other than the one it was first recorded in. I loved that morning, and found several new tales – I was looking for women's stories at the time. As a parting gift they gave me the latest volume in the *Folktales of the Jews* (edited by Dan Ben-Amos) which they had just published in English. A wonderful gift, even if its weight meant I would have to leave a pair of shoes behind so it could go in my suitcase for the flight back. (I have since bought e-book versions of the other volumes, but to be honest, turning the pages and finding a jewel or a stone is far better.)

This started me off. Every trip we went on I looked for the Jewish stories. Some places it was easy – in Cracow, there were books of Jewish legends in every shop. I asked non-Jewish guides of European cities if they knew any, where could I find any stories? And they did, and they told them.

I picked up loads in Prague, apart from the Golem. I visited the Altneuschul, where he is supposed to be still in the attic, waiting. And, do you know, you can't see anything like an attic from the inside, but outside there is a door high up, under the roof tiles…where does it lead? Is he still there?

Soon, I was telling more and more Jewish stories. I was being asked for a Jewish story for this occasion, or that (an invaluable tool is the *Jewish Story Finder* by Sharon Barcan Elswit), and then finding I was adapting them to situations, so they weren't in their original form and yet they were linked to my history. I feel the truth of them as I tell and I'm sure my audiences do too. Now I am learning Yiddish to read more in the *mamaloshen* – mother tongue – as nuances aren't always translated well. Imagine my joy when a story of the men of Chelm came up in class and I was able to read it reasonably OK in Yiddish as I already knew it!

So, like any other storyteller, I listen out for stories, some catch my ear and heart quicker than others. I comb through second-hand bookstalls for a gem, I buy books on line, I read blogs. In short, I do everything I can to find a story and then I cross-check with those I have already to see if it's a version I have and how it is changed. These stories keep me guessing, what will they be about next? Do you know the one that is told by Jews from Afghanistan about Alexander the Great? It's as if he's still invading! Or the one from *Fiddler on The Roof* which has a tale in its brevity: 'May the Lord bless the Tsar and keep him – far away from us!' Or the one about the family that couldn't get on in their house as it was such a squash and a squeeze? The rabbi told them to get more and more people and animals in their house until it was full to bursting. The tales are out there, everywhere.

Kamishibai in Australia

JACKIE KERIN

Kamishibai (kami – paper, shibai – theatre) is a Japanese mode of storytelling. It employs a small narrow stage with an opening on one side so viewers can see a succession of cards revealed as the story is narrated. First appearing in the late 1920s, kamishibai is embedded in a long tradition of picture story telling: it is connected to the illustrated scrolls that priests once used when narrating Buddhist doctrine, and in the present, it is connected to manga (comic books) and anime (animation). Traditional kamishibai storytellers mounted their wooden stages onto the back of their bicycles, and, loaded with story cards and sweets to sell to the children who gathered to hear the stories, took to the streets. I have read that at the height of the fad, there were upwards of 25,000 gaito kamishibai storytellers (street performers).

No one can say who invented kamishibai, for essentially the technique is transmitted directly from person to person and it is currently enjoying a period of revival in storytelling communities in disparate locations across the globe.

I won't say more about the history of kamishibai as a quick search on the Internet will lead you to detailed sites with all you need to know. Instead I will share some of the fun I have had with kamishibai in Australia.

I have always enjoyed visual storytelling and the interplay of image, gesture and music with the oral tradition. It was only a matter of time before my inquisitiveness turned to kamishibai.

My adventures began in 2011. I was working on a folk tale with an unusual protagonist – a dog that had split in two and when he was hastily repaired by his owner, was left with two legs up and two legs down! The Split Dog stories are generally regarded as having roots in Appalachian folk tale but I first met this magical character in Graham Seal's book *Great Australian Stories: Legends, Yarns and Tall Tales*. Determining this story belonged to the people, I decided to create a Split Dog story of my own. After months of shaping the yarn I was left with the problem of helping, children especially, visualise this topsy-turvy dog. I experimented with balloon dogs, but my heart wasn't in it. I mentioned my dilemma to my comic book maker friend, Bernard Caleo. He paused for a moment and then said, 'Kamishibai.'

To cut a long story short, a skilled carpenter friend, Ted Smith, made me a wooden stage from recycled Eucalyptus. He did not want payment but made conditions: one, that when I had my first story, I would tell it at his granddaughter's kindergarten; two, that I take good care of the stage (honourable scars only) and, three, that it not lie idle. I quickly made a thick carry bag (honourable scars only), launched into making the story cards for *Split Dog* and the inaugural performance took place at the kindergarten. For several years I shared the stage with Bernard and it has never been idle.

I think of my storytelling as an art. It is important to me that my props are made by me or other artists, storytellers and illustrators. I don't want to buy props and stories from factories (I have made one exception). I have learned, by trial and error, to make my own cards and experimented with paint, paper cut-outs and water pencils. I have redrawn some card sets, as the first time around I included 'thought bubbles' and 'action lines' (from the language of comics) but decided this was unnecessary as it is the narrator's voice that conveys movement and the inner life of the protagonists.

Technically, I have experimented with a number of bespoke kamishibai stands. I am indebted to my storytelling, camera operator, props maker friend Alex Kharnam, for a stand adapted from a heavy-duty camera tripod that can be raised and lowered and packed away in a suitcase for easy travel. I can be in and out of spaces quick as a flash. I am humbled by the patience of friends who have helped to assemble the many contraptions that preceded Alex's invention. Having solved the problem of a stand, there remained something else I felt impelled to explore.

While l love working in controlled spaces (I have a theatre background), I am drawn to the idea of storytelling in festivals, in tents and on the streets. After spending many hours trawling through images of gaito kamishibai storytellers I decided I wanted to strap a stage to my bicycle. My wooden stage is too precious and too heavy for the task, so using industrial strength cardboard, I built and painted my own bicycle rig. I can ride it to local gigs, take it on a train or I can carry the bike on a rack on the car and assemble it on site. My kamishibai bicycle and I have visited many festivals. And these days, I also decorate the bike with small *Split Dog* comics that I created so children can have the fun of experiencing the connection between kamishibai and comics. I sell these off my bike for a $2 coin.

The adventures that begun in 2011, continue. I like to think that what I do is useful and can spark curiosity and I like to think that the stories I tell, and the way I tell them, may bring people together and I believe that there is great strength in collaboration.

I am currently collaborating with violinist Sarah Depasquale and artist Loraine Callow. The three of us have two projects on the boil: *Tales from*

the Flyway and *The Amazing Case of Dr Ward*. The former is a storytelling piece that contemplates the wonder of migratory birds, those that fly annually from the south-east corner of Australia to Siberia along the East Asian Australasian Flyway. It includes a kamishibai story that was sent as jpegs from Yatsu-higata (a wetland in Japan) to Boondall (a wetland in Queensland) to me. I live by an urban wetland on the Flyway not far from the city of Melbourne. With Sarah's musical score, we tell of the journey of the smallest of the migratory shore birds, the red-necked stint.

A work in development at the time of writing, *The Amazing Case of Dr Ward* explores the transportation of exotic plants to Australia in the 1800s and includes two kamishibai tales, one with original artwork by Loraine and one 'off the shelf' traditional Japanese folk tale, and both are underscored with Sarah's music.

Both my wooden and industrial strength cardboard kamishibai stages have been seen by thousands. I have taken them across Australia and performed internationally. Working solo and with Sarah, I have delivered stories to audiences in theatres, libraries, schools, parks, gardens and tents, and at storytelling, literary and folk festivals.

My aim is simple: to craft and pass on stories that have been thoughtfully created, to the best of my ability. As my repertoire has expanded and I have grown in confidence, I have learned that kamishibai storytelling touches hearts in ways I never imagined.

I encourage you to connect and introduce yourself to others enjoying the kamishibai revival and explore the network of tellers and artists.

Storytellers around the world exchange photographs and news of their adventures on a public Facebook group: The World of Kamishibai.

And treat yourself to a book. I recommend any text by Tara M. McGowan but particularly *The Kamishibai Classroom: Engaging Multiple Literacies Through the Art of 'Paper Theater'*. This book is valuable whether or not you work in schools.

If you would like to make a cardboard rig for your bike like mine, the plans are on my website.

May our paths cross one day and may good ideas be shared.

Be inspired!

Born of this Land

ANNE E. STEWART

Born of this land I am born of this land and it has always been in my blood. From early school holidays to the coast, where the wild seas thrilled me, and the wind-swept dunes nestled my solitary figure. To the territory for three years where I was privy to some of Australia's most spectacular landscapes; where I came to understand the feeling of sacredness of land. A gorge, a waterfall, a sheltered creek bank, sheer cliff faces that reached to the sky demanding as much respect as the mightiest of cathedrals. I am born of this land, it is in my blood.

But the stories of this land are not my stories, yet, and I grow more determined. I know the path will be winding and long, but it is time to make our way through the minefields of hurt and injustice, misappropriation and litigation. It is time to reach out our hand and ask our indigenous brothers and sisters to show us the way. I want my children to hear the stories of the land and as a storyteller I want to help keep the stories alive. It has often been said amongst the storytellers that there are only five basic stories and every other story told or written is a variation of these five. These inner wisdoms have been clothed by many different cultures in ways that pertained to their particular landscape and values.

We share this landscape with indigenous Australians and yet we are looking at it from different angles. But the tide is turning, there is a slow

groundswell and yearning for shared stories. Witness the unifying effects of 'the Australian Story', courtesy of the Olympics and the pride all Australians took in our indigenous culture. We need to move forward together but with a shared dreaming. A dreaming that will sustain our hearts and souls as well as our landscape and environment. But there is still a lot of pain; not only did we take their land and their children, now we try to take their culture. Joseph Wambugu Githhaiga, a Law graduate from Western Australia's Murdoch Universtiy, writes in a thoughtful, lengthy discourse, 'Intellectual Property Law and the Protection of Indigenous Folklore and Knowledge'. He explains the intricate web of associations present in aboriginal folklore and mythology and he argues that to try and protect these intricacies with copyright laws is 'beyond the scope of western private property rights. Indigenous people regard intellectual and real property to be so intimately linked that no meaningful distinction can be made between the two. Indigenous designs... represent the title deeds of land ownership.' In the title of Githhaiga's paper the notion of protectionism reflects the fear of letting go, the fear of losing their culture for someone else's benefit, the reluctance to share their stories.

I feel hurt and ashamed that indigenous Australian's brief history with white fellas has left them so suspicious. In his suggested protocols for reform he states that,

> artists, writers and performers should desist from unauthorised incorporation of indigenous heritage in their works. Instead they should support the artistic and cultural development of indigenous peoples and participate in public awareness campaigns to promote indigenous art and culture.

This indigenous heritage is the heritage of the landscape and before we can walk forward together we must share the stories. As oral historians and storytellers we ask to help with the task. You were once experts in the oral tradition, your storytellers and song men told the tales, but now before they are lost we seek permission, like your apprentices, to help keep the stories alive. As Margaret Read MacDonald says, 'When the legends die, the dream ends. When the dreams end there is no more greatness.'

Aboriginal culture is a dynamic culture and it has changed dramatically since the arrival of the First Fleet in 1788. Where many proud nations once lived on the land, now communities are spread from remote to rural areas; in provincial towns and major cities, they are all culturally distinct and regional names recognise this. For instance, in East Arnhem Land live the Yolgnu people, in Victoria are the Koori's and in Queensland, Murry's live along the east coast, to name a few. The colour of their skin may range from pale cream to dark blue black, like an old fella I had a beer with in the Nhulunbuy Pub. But it's not the colour of your skin that defines you as aboriginal but your sense of identity, your kinships and relation to the land.

I too am born of this land and I long to tell its stories. As a storyteller I have always been aware and respectful of the protocols in telling and receiving aboriginal stories and I bring your attention to a great paper produced by Australian Library and Information System called 'Aboriginal and Torres Strait Islander Protocols for Libraries, Archives and Information Services'. While it doesn't specifically relate to the telling of stories it 'deals with Indigenous intellectual property issues' and acts as a guideline for collecting indigenous material and relating to Aboriginal and Torres Strait Islanders. The guidelines remind us that 'there is information that is restricted, that our children cannot learn about, there is information that is restricted even to adults, there is information that is of a secret or sacred nature, that many people have no knowledge of or access to. That knowledge is only there for certain people to have access to.' (Gularrwuy Yunupingu, 1986)

I accept this restriction but ask only to tell the nursery rhymes, the folk tales. Aboriginal culture, also, has much to teach us about caring for our environment. For too long in the stories (and libraries) ... 'we have been referred to and catalogued as "savages" or "primitive" while Western industrial peoples are referred to as advanced and complex.' (Mick Dodson, 1993) This was brought home to me recently when I was researching a

story to tell at Ballarat Fine Art Gallery. There was a new painting I wanted to tell a story about. A young girl emerges bedraggled from rough emerald green waves capped with frothy white horses. I recollected a story from the old Victorian Readers, Year Four Book, 'A Brave Australian Girl'. Her name was Grace Bussell and she was billed as the Grace Darling of Australia, a similar story told of a young girl in England who had saved the passengers of a floundering vessel off the coast.

In the Australian version she was accompanied by a 'black servant', no name, no identity just a black servant. However, surfing the net, I found the hidden story. The black servant was a thirty-year-old employee of the homestead where Grace lived, and he spotted the ship heading for the reef. His name was Sam Isaacs Yebble and he was the son of an indigenous woman from the Margaret River region and his dad was a native American Indian sailor who had jumped ship. Busselton was named for Grace's family and they're still there running a winery. There's a shared story; aboriginal people, also, must be able to look to the stories with pride, it is us that must look at them in shame at our ignorant forbears. When I look at the question theoretically the task seems ominous, the subject feels heavy, but in reality it's different.

Yesterday, on my birthday, as I waited for my parents to arrive in Ballarat and shout me a 'gourmet' lunch, I decided to head for the Aboriginal Co-operative. I was curious to know if they had any info on the stories of native flowers. I've heard Frances Firebrace tell 'Why the Waratah is red' and I wanted to know if they knew any more. They invited me for a morning cuppa and in joyous spirits we swapped stories. I found out that tall, jovial, smiling Merv had a birthday the following day. I shared my knowledge of the stories of the Wathourong people (the local Tribe), my travels to the territory, my love of great myths and legends. We even talked of training up some of their teenage kids and having them interview some of the elders before it's too late, before the stories disappear.

And it is with a great sense of pride that I report on the issue of telling indigenous stories: 'Well if a black fella's not telling them, I reckon you'd be the next best thing.' Throughout my travels, my interviews with indigenous

tellers for 'Swag' and my insistence on raising the issue, I have found aboriginal people, on the whole, to be incredibly generous of spirit. They approach life with tremendous humour and are always first to make a joke at their own expense. 'Reconciliation' walks in all major capitals have shown the growing support from the wider community, inroads are being made into breaking down the barriers. Shared stories will certainly strengthen these inroads and I look forward to the shared path. After twenty-three years of this storytelling apprenticeship I have a clear direction of the path I wish to follow. Along with the great myths and legends that inform my Celtic inheritance and world mythology, thanks to great folklore collections in libraries I have worked, will stand the stories of our country. In my family we have recently welcomed niece, Aretha Eileen Anne Stewart, born of Paul Stewart of the St Kilda/Elwood clan and Donna Brown of the Gumbaingirr Mob from the Nambucca Heads region of NSW. More than ever I know, as Aretha's indigenous Grandma says, 'Annie, you need to make sure you tell all the stories, for all the kids.'

From the Alps

KLARA MILLER-FUHREN

My name is Klara Miller-Fuhren and I live in a beautiful area at the foot of the German Alps. It is an area historically known to be a centre of Celtic culture more than 2,000 years ago. Celtic people had a special place next to the king reserved only for the storyteller, when the tribes met for big gatherings, called tings. The king ruled and organised and was the leader of the people, the storyteller gave them food for thought and cause for spiritual growth. What made him special was that his words touched the souls of the listeners and opened their hearts for the good, the truthful and the beautiful.

This combination was so powerful that they never had wars over 500 years of their existence. So storytelling has a very long tradition in this area of Upper Bavaria.

Bearing these origins in mind I like to continue following the aims of the ancient art of storytelling.

My introduction to storytelling came rather late in life. I grew up on a farm in Bavaria and I was never told any stories in my parental household. I had to wait till I had children of my own at the age of 40. My son and daughter brought home lots of stories and songs from their nursery schools. At that time my husband and I lived in Holland and were very surprised at how happily our two children took to the songs and stories from their nurseries.

Since I had been an actress in Paris for ten years, long before my marriage, I didn't find it difficult to make my children happy by re-telling the stories they had heard in kindergarten. I was amazed how attentively they listened quietly again and again to the same stories. They seemed to need stories like food and drink. They enjoyed falling asleep at night by listening to my stories. I started with classical fairy stories and also invented some of my own.

At that time, I found professional training for storytellers and it all started for me there and then. During the training I realised that stories have been told throughout history in all countries of the world, but mainly to adults. So, I invented my own programs with stories from China, the Orient, Russia, Europe and so on and organised storytelling for adults. My evenings had titles like 'Stories of Strong Women', 'Stories of Courage and Determination', 'Of Helpful Beings', 'Stories of Courage and Patience', 'Stories of Fortune and Happiness', and so on.

Over the years I deeply understood that stories made people feel good, because the stories echoed something within people, like values that seem to be universal to mankind. My understanding and experience I had gathered over the years I applied to where I live now. Some twenty years ago we moved close to the Alpine Mountains of Bavaria. In this area many clinics provide rehabilitation for people after they had been treated for heart

attack, cancer, artificial hip and knee operations elsewhere. I contacted the local rehabilitation centres and they took to the idea of having storytelling evenings for their patients. With my husband's knowledge of psychotherapy and my big repertoire we looked for topics which could be helpful for severely ill people. Our aim was to make these suffering people feel as good as my children felt listening to stories. We spoke to doctors and therapists about what kind of stories would support the doctors' healing efforts. The understanding emerged that it would be greatly beneficial to people convalescing from severe illnesses to listen to stories that ended happily.

My evenings in the clinics with Happy End stories were received very well. You see, people who had had a heart attack, or treatment for cancer, or new hips put in, experienced a forceful change of fate in their lives. Through all their treatments they were full of fear and questions like: Will I have another heart attack? Will my cancer come back? Will I ever be able to walk again without pain? Doubts and anxiety occupied their thoughts in a great way. And nobody could answer their questions conclusively. Their lives had been turned upside down and openly or secretly they had become victims of rather gloomy outlooks to their future.

How deeply did my stories touch their feelings! In the beginning of the narrating hour they would often sit there stiff and all to themselves, yet fifteen minutes later their eyes began to sparkle, their faces relaxed, and they looked like happiness had arisen in them miraculously. In their weeks and months of treatment they had never experienced an hour like this. When I ended they had rediscovered joy and happiness and hope that their situations might end successfully and happily like in the stories they had just heard.

Using Storytelling to Teach Special Needs Students

GARY AND LINDA KUNTZ

Linda, my wife, teaches functional life skills to special needs (learning disabled) students at a local high school. One of her biggest challenges is that the students have trouble retaining the information taught via traditional teaching methods, which relies heavily on memorization and repetition. Breaking that cycle she now uses a series of activities, storytelling programs, and stories to revise how the curriculum is taught. Using storytelling techniques, she and the other special needs teachers have seen a marked improvement in the amount of information her students retain and how they perform on standardized tests.

A few years ago I was asked to do a storytelling program for her class. This was a new audience for me so I talked with the teachers about what level of stories the students would be able to understand. After some discussion, the teachers decided that the majority of the students had a third grade (7–9-year-old) comprehension level and would be able to understand stories aimed at that age range. The day of the program I arrived at the classroom with a selection of stories for that age range, along with some other stories suitable for a slightly younger or older level.

The first story was one I normally start off with for 3rd–4th grade students. The students in the class followed along with the story, were attentive and made the appropriate responses. In watching their reactions, it appeared they wanted something more – more complexity, more elements from the story. So instead of following the program I had planned, the next story I told was one I use in middle school, 6th–8th grade (11–13-year-olds). Surprising me, the class appeared to understand the story even with the more complex theme. But it was again like they wanted more from the story. So, for the next story, I employed one from the list of stories that would normally be used for high school students, grades 9–12 (ages 14–18). Because of their reactions, how they received and understood the story, the rest of the program were stories that that I would use in a regular high school program.

That evening Linda and I talked about the program and how surprised I and the teachers were at how well the students understood the high school age stories. She had recognized the shift in age levels in the stories and during a break time the teachers had talked about how the students had reacted to the stories. The comprehension of the more complex themes was something unexpected for her and the other teachers and they were uncertain as to how and why that happened. After some discussion, that lasted well into the night, we decided that because most of the students in that class didn't read, or didn't read well, they were used to gathering and processing information mainly through listening. Because they were just listening, without a television or other type of screen showing them how they should react, they could put themselves into the stories. And so were able to understand them based upon their capabilities and not those of others.

I was asked to come back the next month to tell Halloween stories for the class. I said yes, but, based upon my experience with the last storytelling program, I would tell the same stories I would use for a regular high school or adult program. The program went well: one teacher (my wife) walked out before one story she dislikes, called Rats in the Graveyard, (it has a happy ending, for the rats) and another teacher jumped out of her chair during a different story, but the class followed along and appeared to like the stories.

After the program, I was talking with the lead teacher about how well the students followed along with the stories when a student came up to us. The teacher asked him what he wanted, and he turned to me and said, 'Mr Kuntz, I liked those stories you told today but I really liked the one from last time.' When I asked which story, he proceeded to tell me the story he heard a month ago. This isn't an uncommon occurrence for a storyteller if they have been in the same place multiple times, so I didn't think anything of it. I told him that he did a good job telling it and that he should continue to tell the story to others. When he left I noticed the teacher was looking at him with a quizzical expression on her face. I told her that he had remembered that story pretty well and she said, 'Yes, but he can't remember his home address or telephone number from week to week.' Yet he had remembered and told a story he had heard from over a month ago.

That night Linda and I went over what had happened with that student. We knew there was something in the story format that caused that student to remember that particular story. It somehow bypassed his learning disability and allowed him to retain that information. Since the student who remembered and retold the story was one of her life-skill students she decided to try a different method for teaching him his address.

The standard teaching method focused on repetition and memorization where they would have the students repeat their address several times throughout the day. Those students that could write would write it down. This was a daily exercise each school day. For about half of the students this method worked, they could remember their address and telephone number. But for the other half, they would have to start over again each Monday. Linda wondered whether using a story to teach the address would help that student remember it, so she created this story and told it next day in the class:

I wanted to go trick or treating at your house on Halloween, but I got lost. I was dressed in my very best alligator costume and was heading to your house when I realized I left your address at home. Since it was late I didn't want to go back, besides, I knew I could remember it because we had practiced it at school. It was really dark and every once in a while, I thought I heard something behind me. It was like something was following me. When I turned around I could almost see something and got scared. Then I realized it was only my imagination and thought to myself 'I'm just being silly'. Besides what spook would be brave enough to mess with a big alligator?

It was so late that only the big kids were still trick or treating, so I knew I had to hurry. Then I came to the corner of two streets, Pine and Maple. I knew your street was named after a tree, but I had forgotten which one. Was it the Pine Christmas tree or was it the big Maple shade tree? I couldn't remember, which one could it be? I looked and looked at the two street signs trying to remember the name of the street. Pine or Maple, Maple or Pine, which one could it be? Finally, I decided it must be Maple, that big shade tree, and started walking down Maple Street.

At this point in the telling, the student blurted out, 'No, Mrs Kuntz, that's the wrong street. It's Pine Street.'

'Are you sure?' I asked. 'Because I think it's Maple?' and he replied, 'No, it's the Christmas tree street, Pine Street.'

'Okay, if you are sure I'll go down Pine Street.'

Finally, I decided it must be Pine, the Christmas tree street, and started walking down Pine Street.

I could see the houses with their lights on so I could see the numbers and was looking for, oh what was that number? Was it 1142, or was it 1147, or maybe it was 1148? I knew it had to be one of them and hoped it wasn't 1142 because that house looked spooky. It was big and looked dark, even with the front light on. There were big cobwebs hanging from the porch roof and I thought 'How big is the spider that made those cobwebs?' But it might be the correct house, so I started walking down the sidewalk to that spooky front door.

At this point the student blurted out again, 'No, Mrs Kuntz, that's the wrong house!'

Again, a dialog outside of the story – 'Are you sure, because I thought your house number was 1142?'

He said, 'My house doesn't have any cobwebs on the porch. Besides those are fake, you get them at the store, there aren't any big spiders anyway.'

'But I can read the numbers under the porch light: 1142. How do you know those aren't your numbers?'

He said, 'Because I can read my numbers under my porch light.'

'Really? What do they say?'

He said, 'They say 1, 1, 4, 7,' slowly reading them in his mind's eye.

'Are you sure?'

'Yes!'

'Okay, I'll change the story.'

So, I was looking at the three house numbers and then remembered it was 1147! I didn't have to go to 1142 and deal with the cobwebs! I found

the house with 1147 on it and went skipping happily down the sidewalk to the front door. I knocked on the door and said, 'Trick or Treat'.

'Do you know who came to the door?' I asked.
    'It was me!' he said.
    'Yes, it was you at what house?'
    '1147!' he replied.

I got my treats and skipped back down the sidewalk. So, remember, if you ever see an alligator skipping down the sidewalk in your neighborhood say hi because it might be me.

After hearing and participating in that story the student could remember his address when asked for the remainder of the year.

Over the last few years Linda has been using more storytelling techniques and stories to teach her students. Some guidelines we developed for these stories are:

- The story has to be specific to the subject being taught. Don't try to teach multiple lessons in the same story. (In the address story she didn't try to teach the telephone number within the address story.)
- It cannot be presented as a standard classroom lesson. 'Standard' meaning where the teacher stands at the front of the classroom teaching a lesson. Instead, the lesson is part of the story.
- It must be vivid to allow the audience to 'see' the story.
- It must be interactive, allowing the students to participate in and even to change the story.

Using storytelling techniques and following the story guidelines has given Linda and the other special needs teachers a tool they use on a daily basis to teach their students. Most of the times the stories are short and are created on the fly, as needed for that lesson, or for a specific student. Sometimes it is a longer, more involved story when multiple students are involved. It can be more work and require more creativity from the teacher, but the results are worth it.

Sharing Stories, Sharing Understanding: Learning Language through Story

EIRWEN MALIN

One lovely May morning a storyteller walked happily along in the sunshine looking forward to sharing his stories at the town library. Perhaps because the spring weather had tempted everyone out of doors, or perhaps for some other reason, when he arrived at the library everything was ready, but there was no audience. A storyteller without anyone to listen is a sad storyteller, but someone saved the day. 'Let's take you to a class,' she said. 'English for Speakers of Other Languages (ESOL).' When they reached the class the storyteller quickly decided to tell a story from Wales.

He told the story, and as soon as he had finished one of the group said, 'We have a story like that in my country,' and briefly recounted it. 'I have a story from my country,' said another, and she told that one, and so the class went on with learners telling stories from their own traditions and the storyteller, who knew lots of stories, setting off new threads. The learners who came from many different countries and backgrounds were amazed by the similarities in the stories coming from such different places.

The ESOL tutor was pleased with how her students has listened so carefully and understood the stories told in English, but even more pleased that they had been motivated to use the English they had learned to tell stories from their own cultures. Her learners were so engaged and so willing to speak that she wished she could have a storyteller in class more often.

Now the storyteller, who was David Ambrose, Artistic Director of Beyond the Border, Wales' International Storytelling Festival, was also very happy and he told others how he and the learners had shared their stories. Knowing that I was interested in storytelling too, one of the people he told was me. At that time I was working for NIACE Cymru (the National Institute for Adult Continuing Education working in Wales) and the work that made the ;Sharing Stories: Sharing Understanding; project a reality began.

Those of us who love stories know that telling and hearing stories is a fundamental method of human communication in all known human cultures. Academics suggest that storytelling has evolutionary origins and that human brains are specially tuned to attend to stories. Maintaining attention produces brain changes that focus our understanding and improve our memory of the content. The 'Sharing Stories: Sharing Understanding' project focused on stories as a way of helping migrants learn English. It was designed to use traditional stories that often have themes common to many cultures. They often have repetitious structures that give extra support to language learning, and opportunities for listeners to join in with the story. Well known stories such as Stone Soup, The Tailor's Jacket and The Rock were commonly used, along with many others which would be familiar to storytellers.

The project was aimed at migrants to Wales, who had limited English, to support them in gaining confidence to learn English. In doing so they would improve their employability, access to a number of services such as health, education, commercial services and improve their wellbeing. At the same time, they would be able to learn, through stories, about their host culture in Wales and about the many cultures represented by their fellow migrants from different parts of the world. In all, participants from around thirty different countries were involved. The project focused on the early stages of language learning and in particular on encouraging learners to speak aloud. Learners with good understanding can often be reluctant to speak; encouraging the sharing of stories inspired them to overcome their lack of confidence. Whilst this project was entirely concerned with learning English, the lessons learned could be applied to the development of any language. Wales has two languages and though the project activities were predominantly in English, participants were pleased to hear some Welsh language as part of the activities and were keen to learn more.

A notable factor in this project was the use of professional storytellers. This cultivated an environment which privileged the spoken word rather than the written. With a large repertoire of stories to hand, the storytellers were able to respond to themes and ideas that arose from each group as required, so sessions were able to be very flexible. As they were always working with an ESOL specialist who was able to capture and reinforce the language learning from the interactions, none of the rigour of more traditional language learning methods was lost. The performance skills of the storyteller made it easier for listeners to understand stories even if they did not understand every word, and their confidence in their own learning improved. When the ESOL tutor then reinforced the vocabulary or grammar encountered learners were responsive.

NIACE Cymru (now the Learning and Work Institute), an adult learning charity, and Beyond the Border brought their combined skills to devise and resource the project, which was funded by the Big Lottery Fund in Wales, People and Places Programme. To ensure that the project reached its intended audience we worked with five community organisations in Cardiff and Swansea. It was designed to develop practice, and storytellers and ESOL tutors were encouraged to explore new ideas and delivery methods. Successful practice was shared across the project.

Two styles of group evolved. Firstly, a more structured 6- or 10-week 'course' with the same group of learners attending regularly, and secondly a more structured approach with a lesson plan devised in advance. For very new learners, this was the best approach. However, for others, work or family demands made a regular commitment difficult and a drop-in type of group was used. These sessions worked more like a story circle, with the storyteller starting the session with a story and then inviting learners to contribute. In the early days of these groups only more confident learners contributed but as the weeks progressed others were motivated to share their story, sometimes partly in English and partly in their first language, or with help from another learner. Some would sing something or recite a poem and the sessions became very popular social events as well as learning sessions. The welcoming and supportive atmosphere that was maintained encouraged even the shyest contributors.

The project was deliberately structured to include some more social, intercultural events partly organised by the learners themselves, which made them feel respected and welcome to Wales and provided the opportunity to celebrate and share their own cultures through stories in English for all nationalities to hear. These social events were open to a wider audience from the local community and were well attended. Two groups of learners, one from Cardiff and one from Swansea, were also able to visit the 2014 Beyond the Border Festival and had an afternoon of stories, finishing with the very Welsh tradition of tea and cake in Milgi's café.

Over the lifespan of the project eight storytellers worked with ESOL tutors and nearly 400 learners in short courses. Nearly all (88 per cent) became confident to understand a short story in English and over a third gained sufficient confidence to tell a story in English to a small group of people. It was the way that the stories motivated learners to speak in English that was possibly the most noteworthy learning point from the project. Frequently ESOL learners have a good understanding but are unconfident in speaking. Possibly because the focus for their speaking out was stories from their own traditions, material that was culturally familiar to them, they seemed to gain in confidence. Project participants varied in nature, with one young woman arriving in Britain only a week before she and her young daughter joined a session and others who were long-term residents whose confidence in English was still low even after many years.

Storytellers and ESOL tutors kept detailed notes of the stories used, how they were delivered, successful exercises and the development of individual learners' understanding and confidence to speak. Successful techniques of telling, confidence-building exercises and other practice was shared

throughout the project and has been collected in a publication, *Sharing Stories: Sharing Understanding*, which also contains text versions of some of the favourite stories used in the project and a DVD of 'tellings' recorded within the project. The book also includes some background material and more detailed analysis of the use of particular stories. It is available from Beyond the Border via the website www.beyondtheborder.com/publications/

Storytelling to Enable Language

CHRISTINE WILLISON

One of the most rewarding things I have done as a storyteller is to work with people whose first language is not English, helping them to understand sentence construction, the musicality of language and to extend vocabulary. During the 1980s I did a weekly session in the German department of the University of East Anglia, helping students to gain a better understanding of language. The joy of stories is universal and in no time at all I had students joining in the call-and-response aspects of story and providing repeated phrases.

Similarly in special schools working with children/young people with almost no written and limited spoken skills, the art of oral storytelling gave opportunities to discover student's capabilities and understanding, together with the fun and joy of language.

More recently I was invited to participate in the project described above by its enabler Eirwen Malin, which enabled refugees and asylum seekers to access the English language through storytelling. I was asked to work with a group of women in tandem with an ESOL teacher. The women were from many places and had varying degrees of English language.

After several weeks we had noticeable progress. By the end of the project I had the pleasure of watching groups of people telling stories to each other.

I am currently working with a Kurdish Syrian family who, when they arrived in the UK as refugees, had almost no English. I worked with two ESOL teachers who started with simple words, days of the week, the time of day and so on. It was then my turn. I told a simple tale of an old woman and a magpie. Using artefacts, mime and drawing on a flipchart, the looks on their smiling faces told me that there was understanding, amusement and some relief from the more formal style of teaching.

In the second week I could see real progress, there was more language from them, less reticence and a greater willingness to have a go. After the formal teaching I told a simplified version of The Little Red Hen, again using drawings and artefacts from my basket which included some wheat (clipped from a field the day before), two stones, to demonstrate grinding, a small bag of flour and a loaf. The recognition was heart-warming. At the end of my session I presented them with the loaf which I had baked the day before. Bread is symbolic of friendship and sharing in many cultures.

For my third session I told Little Red Riding Hood, with the aid of a doll, which was easily transformed from Little Red Riding Hood into Grandma and then into a wolf. It caused plenty of amusement. There was recognition of the basket, which in this case contained apples for Grandma, because last week it had contained a loaf, recognition of the colour red and much more. I perceived an even greater understanding of language.

Next, I told Stone Soup, bringing a stone, an onion, a potato and a carrot, together with some herbs, a saucepan, some water and a wooden spoon out of my basket. In this instance I told the story at the start of the session and the ESOL teachers used words and phrases from my story for further work. I presented the family with bunches of herbs from my garden.

For the fifth session, armed with the knowledge that the husband/father was going to be doing some voluntary work at our local garden centre, I told the story of Jack the Giant Killer. This time I used vernacular, kept the flow of the story, started with 'Once Upon A Time', even though these words were difficult for the family. I was keen for them to hear the musicality of story/language.

With much mime, and objects such as a bag of beans, drawings and actions, they were soon on track. Following the story, I drew out of my basket six flowerpots, a bag of compost, some sticky labels and the bag of beans. I asked them to write their children's and their own names on the labels, then stick them on the pots, ready to take home and share both the story and the activity with the rest of the family.

Since then the family have proudly shown me a photograph of their bean plants.

For the next session I was asked to use some tools, hammer, nails and such. I spent some time racking my brains and eventually decided on The Shoemaker and the Elves. This time my trusty basket contained some leather, scissors, a hammer and some nails. We were able to explore the story through these artefacts and with the aid of drawings. The ESOL teacher followed the story by getting the family to answer questions about it and to do a version of hangman providing letters for a word from the story. Storytelling was now becoming the main focus for language and the ESOL teachers were becoming storytellers themselves.

The Three Little Pigs caused much amusement; the woman learner has been using 'huff' and 'puff' in other language sessions following the story.

Next, I used The Owl and The Pussycat and, despite the nonsense words, the family enjoyed the rhyming – honey and money, boat and five-pound

note, etc. The music of language is being heard, and resonances with their own language and poetry are recognised.

All simple stuff, we are but building language relevant to their new lives. Good preparation is key to this activity, relevance is hugely important. So, if you are invited to do similar work, start simple, choose stories containing recognisable objects and have fun.

'Speaking in Tongues': Telling Stories in Languages Other than One's Mother Tongue

FIONA COLLINS

As my storytelling practice, I choose to tell traditional tales. I share, in my own words, stories from the rich store of the oral tradition which, when told in English, begin 'Once upon a time', when told in Welsh, *Amser maith yn ôl* (A long time ago).

Telling a story, by my definition at least, depends on the spoken word to transmit its meaning.[1] Facial expression, gesture, body language and cadence all amplify, interpret and bring to life the words, but the narrative thread, the details of the story, and often its beauty, are carried by the spoken words of the storyteller.[2]

As a storyteller living and working in Wales, a bilingual country, I know that pretty well all of us who live here, including people who don't consider themselves Welsh speakers, are somewhere on a continuum between understanding only 'road sign Welsh' and being totally bilingual. Because of my lively interest in the spoken word and oral communication, I find the connections and tensions between the two tongues of Wales endlessly fascinating.

Because of this awareness, and in order to enter as fully as possible into the storytelling culture of Wales, I decided to make Welsh my second language. I began learning in 1999, and I have worked hard to reach a good standard, but I cannot tell stories in Welsh with the same fluency, ease of expression and rich vocabulary that are available to me, almost without my being aware of it, in my mother tongue.

Nonetheless, I accept almost every invitation I receive to tell in Welsh and bilingually in community settings, which are where I mostly work. This might mean telling to other Welsh learners, to children in Welsh medium schools, to groups of adult first language Welsh speakers or to mixed audiences of Welsh speakers and non-Welsh speakers. I believe that by taking on this challenge, I show my respect for the language. I hope that the delights of hearing Welsh used in the craft of storytelling, even by a non-native speaker, outweigh my deficiencies.

Working for the charity Read for Good, I regularly offer storytelling sessions on the children's wards at Ysbyty Gwynedd, the NHS hospital in Bangor. Here I tell stories – mostly one-to-one – at patients' bedsides, and it can be hard to pick the right language to use. I may spend half an hour talking to a teenager in English, only later to hear him or her respond in fluent Welsh to a Welsh-speaking nurse. Conversely, I might greet a family in Welsh, to be told: 'Sorry, we don't speak Welsh.' Though the first is irritating, the second seems more grave, for the last thing I want to do, as a spoken word practitioner, is to make anyone feel they are 'talking wrong'.

There is a real linguistic richness available to the people of this bilingual nation. It is fascinating, but it creates complexity, as this one example, above, can show.

I realised that there are global implications of my interest in the two tongues of Wales when I watched a TED talk called 'The importance of mother tongues in social cohesion'.[3] The speaker discussed the value of being bilingual in building people's confidence to conceptualise, use and understand language, and in enabling members of minority communities to play a full part in society. It showed me that there are broad applications of my view that multi-lingual provision in storytelling in Wales is important.

This holds true not only here in bilingual Wales, where Welsh speakers, though they may be numerically a minority, are supported by the legal status of the country as bilingual. There are many other settings around the world where people, whether through choice or necessity, live among others with whom they do not share a mother tongue, and where use of their first language is sometimes neither supported nor encouraged. Storytellers working in inner-city areas around the UK will certainly be engaged with this issue.

My favourite story on this topic, which I often tell in Welsh to Welsh learners, goes as follows:[4]

A cat was settling her kittens down to sleep. Cosy and well-fed, they snuggled around her.

But just as they were drifting off to sleep the peaceful scene was shattered by a dog, racing towards them barking and growling. Its ears were up, its tail was up, its eyes blazed and its teeth gleamed. The kittens were terrifed.

The cat did what any mother of any kind anywhere around the world would do: she defended her young. She jumped to her feet and set herself between them and the dog.

She looked the dog right in the eyes, opened her mouth ... and barked.

Now it was the dog's turn to be terrified. Its ears went down, its tail went down, it closed its eyes, it closed its mouth. It turned tail and ran away.

The kittens gazed adoringly at their brave mother.

'Now then, children,' she said to them briskly, 'I hope you can see why it is so important to be able to speak more than one language.'

As well as choosing stories with such messages, what can you, as a storyteller, do to support listeners whose first language is not the same as yours?

First and foremost, don't forget that traditional stories are a great vehicle for understanding and developing language. Rhymes and stories help children to learn to communicate in their mother tongues, and can do the same for all language learners. The pattern of three, and the predictability of traditional narratives, are examples that help to convey important ideas and to increase vocabulary.

Obviously, there is no substitute for total fluency in a language, and not many storytellers will be able to give to learning an additional language the dedication of Michael Harvey, who spent every morning for a year and a half on an intensive Welsh course, and then followed it with a further year and a half of studying two evenings a week at the University of Wales in Cardiff, combined with teaching Welsh to other learners, in order to reach his present impressive facility with Welsh (to say nothing of French or Portuguese, which he also speaks fluently).

One thing, however, which should be well within all storytellers' reach, and which shows respect for both the language from which a story comes and the speakers of that language, is to pronounce names correctly. Seek out a native speaker, in person or through the Internet, and practise getting your tongue around unfamiliar sounds. It will be much appreciated by your listeners.

If you are telling Welsh material, a helpful resource is to be found on the website of Gwilym Morus-Baird,[5] where you can listen to soundclips of names from the Four Branches of the Mabinogion, and even email him to request that he puts up a name you need to practise. There is nothing better than hearing a native speaker's pronunciation, as I have discovered through trying to give written pronunciation guides in my folk tale books.

Another strategy, which I think is both helpful and simple, is to seek out and learn traditional openings and closings for stories in different

languages. To hear even a snippet of their mother tongue can be very affirming for listeners, and especially if it comes at the beginning of the story, you have established a connection right from the start. Furthermore, do not underestimate the value to people who do not speak a certain language of hearing it used. Here in Wales I often find a great hunger among non-Welsh speakers to hear Welsh, and most take a great delight in this. This is more than simply cultural tourism. As a Welsh learner myself, I believe I can be an important role model to non-Welsh speakers who either do not want to, or think they are unable to, learn Welsh.

Here, to get you started, are some traditional openings that I use:

Amser maith yn ôl / A long time ago		Welsh
Il y avait une fois / There was once		French
Es war einmal / There was once		German
C'era una volta / There was one time		Italian
Davneem davno[6] / Long and long ago		Russian

Thirdly, if there are speakers of languages that you don't speak among your listeners, draw on their expertise to help you. Of course, this has to be done sensitively, without embarrassing or singling out someone who would prefer, for whatever reason, to keep a low profile. However, it can be very empowering to be asked to be the expert on something which is a fundamental part of your identity. As a bonus, other speakers of that language will almost certainly also be delighted to hear it.

My favourite example of this from my own experience actually concerns not another language, but another register of my mother tongue, English. Years ago, while I still lived in London, I was booked to do a storytelling day in a notoriously tough secondary school, which was in the process of being 'turned around' by a new, dynamic Black headteacher, who had been born in Jamaica and came to the UK at the age of 7. He was later knighted for his services to education.

I can't remember which of us had the idea, but we decided to team-tell the Anansi stories I had planned, with me whispering to him Anansi's direct speech, and him then performing the words in Jamaican patois. The students, who had only ever heard him speak in the formal register of Standard English, were electrified to hear him using what they thought of as 'their' street-talk. It was a thrilling experience to be part of, and created a strong bond between the teacher and his pupils which I'm sure they all remembered for a long time.

Language is the medium of our craft as storytellers. As Marshall McLuhan famously said, 'the medium is the message'. By 'the message', he intended a change that is effected in inter-personal dynamics.[7] As storytellers, our listeners are crucially important to us: without them, we cannot practise our craft – unlike a musician, who can gather an audience by simply beginning to play, I need the attention of at least one listener before I can start to speak.

When we work with stories, we need to be as mindful as possible in our language choices: working in bilingual settings has really awakened me to the subtleties of both my mother tongue and other languages.

It has also made me much more aware of the deep structure of language. I can now see that expressions which come naturally to a first language speaker's lips may be opaque to a listener who is not fluent in the language. In both English and Welsh, native speakers elide words to create a natural rhythm in their speech. Simple expressions like 'I don't know / *Wn i ddim*' can really flummox a non-fluent speaker, and sometimes a more formal, fuller form of words can be helpful. So, I might say 'I do not know / *Dwi ddim yn gwybod*' to help learners keep pace.

Colour and life come to a language through imagery, and these images can be very culturally specific. Where in English one might describe a fierce rainstorm by saying 'it's raining cats and dogs', in Welsh the same idea is conveyed by '*mae hi'n bwrw hen wragedd a ffyn* / it's raining old women and sticks'. To a non-native speaker, both are equally illogical, and may need clarifying. However, I would never suggest avoiding the use of such expressions when you are telling stories, for they bring the language, its speakers and their culture vividly to life.

By telling stories in Welsh or bilingually, I can give the message that I value the Welsh language and, by implication, the culture from which it comes. For me, this is part of honouring the story and the craft of storytelling.

Notes

I am very grateful to Amy Douglas and Ed Fisher for their help in improving this chapter. The shortcomings, sadly, remain all my own.

1   I don't mean to imply here that stories cannot be told in BSL and other languages of the Deaf community. I am just trying to distinguish what I do from other uses of the term 'storytelling', which describe film-making, writing, etc.

2   There is, of course, also a wide and exciting range of traditional ways of supporting traditional storytelling through puppets, objects, shadow screens, crankies, khavads and so on, all of which are valuable in situations where extra provision is helpful in enabling listeners to engage with a story. This is a separate subject.

3   TED talk: www.youtube.com/watch?v=9asuUem0rGs
    De l'importance des langues maternelles pour la cohesion: Marie Rose Moro (accessed 2/6/2017)

4   My thanks go to the late Tony Aylwin, from whom I first heard this story, though with a different cast of creatures. I generally tell it with soft toys, to help learners follow the story, and my version is adapted to the puppets I had!

5   Gwilym Morus-Baird's websites: https://welshmythology.com/resources/ https://mwncinel.com/

6   This is my own transliteration from the Cyrillic alphabet.

7   McLuhan, Marshall, *Understanding Media: The Extensions of Man*, New York: McGraw Hill, 1964. I have drawn on an article (accessed 13/10/17) by Mark Federman of the McLuhan Programme for this definition: http://individual. utoronto.ca/markfederman/article_mediumisthemessage.htm

'Think in the Long Way'

UNCLE LARRY WALSH

'I'm going home, not necessarily straight home. Ride with me, I'm going another way. It might take a little bit of time, but I'll get there.'

Uncle Larry Walsh, January 2018.

I first met Uncle Larry about eight years ago, when he came to a storytelling session of mine at Footscray (Melbourne) Library. My oldest daughter had been working with him, as an artist in support of Aboriginal rights. This piece is the result of an interview conducted in Melbourne on a recent visit. We met at my daughter's house. He was a delight to interview since he didn't require questions to spark off reminiscences and stories. A cup of tea and a comfy chair, along with a fan to reduce the uncomfortable January heat, were all that was needed.

For Uncle Larry, the oral tradition is an important expression of Aboriginal culture. He wishes to display that Aboriginal people live as much in the modern world as intimately as they are connected to their past.

He has been an activist all his life and many projects would not have been set up without his energy; community radio in Victoria, a youth housing project, Elders services, and an Aboriginal community centre to name but a few. He has been instrumental in celebrating Aboriginal history by helping the campaign for the return of cultural and skeletal material to its rightful place.

He was persuaded to join the legal service of the local authority, to help establish citizenship rights for Aboriginal people. But after some successes he left the service because he found working in an organisation and the level of thinking required was too restricting. He had to go away and 'just do the job' so that he could 'think in the long way' like the Uncles and Aunties. Elders in Aboriginal communities are called uncle and auntie as a term of respect.

As a young man wanting to expand his understanding of culture Larry consulted with an elder, who shared some old stories of his place. When he died Larry took over, teaching the stories to young people. The Kulin nation is an alliance of five Indigenous Australian tribes in south central Victoria, Australia. Their collective territory includes Melbourne. Before British colonisation, the tribes spoke five related languages.

He would use some of the languages of the Kulin people to give a better idea of the history and to preserve the languages. His intention was that young people would relate the stories to their families because at the time nobody was talking about Australian Aboriginal stories and relating them to actual historical events.

Without pausing for breath Uncle Larry told me the story about how Koala lost his tail.

Once upon a time Koala and his friend Kangaroo were incredibly thirsty. Koala told Kangaroo that he was so thirsty he thought he might die.

Kangaroo told Koala that they could not give up, they were warriors. He had heard of a river beyond the mountains, with any luck they might find a waterhole in the river bed.

After two days journeying in blistering heat, they came to what was once a fast-flowing river. Koala asked, 'where are these waterholes?'

'Don't despair,' said Kangaroo, 'my mother told me that all you have to do is dig a hole in the right spot in the riverbed and you will find water.' Koala asked Kangaroo to start digging because he was too tired. He went to sleep and while he slept Kangaroo dug a very deep hole in the riverbed. After a while Kangaroo was exhausted and he woke Koala to carry on digging whilst he had a rest. Koala asked if Kangaroo had found water. 'No, not yet,' said Kangaroo. Koala said he was too tired to dig and went back to sleep.

Kangaroo felt sorry for his friend and carried on digging. After much heavy digging, Kangaroo felt the earth get damp and eventually at the bottom of a deep hole he found water. Kangaroo excitedly woke his friend and offered to bring him some water.

Koala woke up, pushed Kangaroo out of the way and dived into the hole, drinking as much as he could without any regard for his friend Kangaroo.

Kangaroo was so angered by this selfish behaviour that he took his stone knife, jumped into the water, stretched out koala's tail and cut it off.

Koala cried out in pain, turned and saw Kangaroo with the knife, jumped out of the hole and ran away. Kangaroo was left to enjoy the water and Koala was left without a tail.

When the 26,000-year-old skeletal remains of the koala were found and investigated, scientists could see that the bones were stressed, exhibiting brown discolouration, which indicated that the animals were suffering from drought conditions. Clearly there were no written records of what

happened 26,000 years ago, but the lack of water is related in many ancient Aboriginal stories, recalling a moral and spiritual meaning together with historical fact.

Uncle Larry explained that the stories are not just words, but include dance, music and visual art. 'You learn the light if you know the whole story.' Aboriginals were prevented in the past from sharing the stories and from practising the dance part of the story. The stories also relate to names, and people are connected to stories through their names.

People are named after birds, animals, reptiles and plants. There is always a story about how you are named. By the time you matured, the elders observed your abilities and your name could be changed, although your original name would remain your official family name. Your abilities such as tracking, healing or storytelling would be reflected in your name. Your name may reflect a tree, since a tree was once a person who performed a truly good deed. Uncle Larry can claim Crow and the associated Raven as his spiritual name.

'People find their way home if they are lost, through the old stories. They find their unique path.'

Uncle Larry tells the story of Bunjil, a creator deity and ancestral being, sometimes depicted as an Eaglehawk. He is one half of the ancestry of the Kulin Nation, regarded as one of two 'moiety' (Aboriginal kinship or clan) ancestors, the other being Waa the crow:

Bunjil has two wives and a son who is Binbeal the rainbow. His brother is Balayang the bat. He is assisted by six *wirmums* or shamans, who represent the clans of the Eaglehawk moiety: Djurt-djurt, the nankeen kestrel; Thara, the quail hawk; Yukope, the parakeet; Dantum, the parrot, Tadjeri, the brushtail possum; and Turnong, the gliding possum.

After creating the mountains, rivers, flora, fauna and laws for humans to live by, Bunjil gathered his wives and sons then asked Crow, who had charge of the winds, to open his bags and let out some wind. Crow opened a bag in which he kept his whirlwinds, creating a cyclone that uprooted trees. Bunjil asked for a stronger wind, and Bunjil and his people were blown up into the sky. Bunjil himself became the star Altair and his two wives, the black swans, became stars on either side.

A Bunurong story (Bunurong, are a Kulin people, on whose native lands Melbourne was built):

> The story tells of a time of conflict among the Kulin nations, when people argued and fought with one another, neglecting their families and the land. The mounting chaos and disunity angered the sea, which began to rise until it had covered the plains and threatened to flood the entire country. Animals fought with each other. Many were killed.
>
> The people went to Bunjil and asked him to help them stop the sea from rising. Bunjil agreed to do so, but only if the people would change their ways and respect the laws and each other. So Bunjil flew down full of anger and started to sing and dance around the moon. He laid feathers on a swan who had been overcome by fighting. Then Bunjil sang the feathers until finally the bird was covered with feathers and was healed. He became the first Black Swan and this is why the nation of Victoria and Australia is black. The next time you see a black swan look carefully. When you ruffle some feathers, you see a few white ones left from the time before he fought. And you will notice that he's big and his feet are red from the blood that stained him after the fight.
>
> Bunjil then walked out to the sea, raised his spear and ordered the water to stop rising.

Suggested Reading

http://footscrayarts.com/profile/uncle-larry-walsh/

How We Got Fire by Uncle Larry Walsh on Vimeo:

https://vimeo.com/130711753

https://www.wheelercentre.com/people/uncle-larry-walsh

Cath and Ramy Share Stories

CATH LITTLE AND RAMY

Cath and Ramy met when Cath was teaching 'English through Storytelling' and Ramy was learning English. Cath soon found out that Ramy was a wonderful storyteller. So Ramy learned English from Cath and Cath learned stories from Ramy. A good swap!

Ramy is originally from Iran, he came to Britain as a political refugee in 2013 and has now been given leave to remain here. He works as a lorry driver. Cath is from Cardiff and works as a storyteller.

Here the two have a conversation about stories.

Cath: How did the 'English through Storytelling' lessons help you learn?

Ramy: They helped me a lot, because when you listen to a story it is interesting. You want to know what is going to happen next. You pay attention to each word and each word stays in your mind. The meaning of the word stays in your mind and each time you remember that story you remember the word in English. One time I wanted to tell you a story and I didn't know the word for hedgehog. Once you told me the word I always remembered it because it was in a story that was important to me.

Cath: I really love that hedgehog story. Who did you hear it from?

Ramy: I had an uncle, a very educated man, he went to Tehran University, the best in the country. He read everything and was curious about everything. When he came to visit he would always say to my brothers and sisters and me, 'Come here, I want to tell you a story'. Every story he told us had some meaning for us. He was teaching us through the stories, teaching us to see life from another point of view.

Once he asked me 'Who is the strongest animal in the jungle?' and I said, 'The lion is!' That's when he told us the story of the hedgehog and that made me think about things in another way. It made me curious. It made me wonder. Another time I told him I wasn't doing very well at school and I wasn't very clever. That's when he told me the story of the Stone Cutter. Do you remember that one?

Cath: Yes, the Stone Cutter is sad because he isn't strong and powerful, so he wishes to be a king. When he finds that the sun is stronger than a king he wishes to be the sun, then a cloud, then a mountain. When he is a mountain he realises that a Stone Cutter is more powerful than a mountain!

Ramy: Yes, the Stone Cutter didn't know how powerful he really was. After that he believed in himself. That's why my uncle told me that story. He wanted me to explore and discover my own power. My uncle's stories were very effective. Me, my brothers and sisters all learned from them and now we are all very independent people and we think for ourselves.

Cath: What's your favourite story?

Ramy: I heard a story that I've never forgotten. It was about a man who was Native American Indian. He lived in a community with white people and they all treated him badly. They didn't accept him. They were racist. But the man just got on with his life. He was tough. In the end something terrible happened, there was a disaster and the man saved the people, but in saving them he lost his own life. He was a hero.

Cath: That's a sad story. I wished he could have lived and the people could have thanked him and been sorry for the way they had treated him.

Will you tell me the story about the hedgehog again?

Ramy: Of course! Once upon a time there was a lion who was king of the jungle. He was a cruel tyrant and he ruled the jungle by bullying and threatening the other animals. He had two assistants – the tiger and the wolf – and they did his nasty work for him. The animals were fed up and frightened and they wished they could get rid of their cruel lion king. The animals all got together and discussed what they should do. They had to get rid of the lion king. One day a hedgehog turned up in the jungle. He told the animals that he would be their new king. The animals all thought that the hedgehog would make a better king, so they sent a message to the lion telling him they had found a new king. When the lion heard the message, he sent the wolf to find out what was happening. When the wolf came to see hedgehog, hedgehog curled himself up into a round ball and he rolled this way and that way. When the wolf put out his paw to touch him, 'Ouch!' he got some prickles in his paw. The wolf went back to the lion and asked to see a doctor. So next the lion sent the tiger. The same thing happened to the tiger and he came back crying with a paw full of prickles. At last the lion went himself to see the hedgehog and the same thing happened to him. Hedgehog was the strongest and so the animals made the hedgehog king. But the hedgehog turned out to be an even worse king than the lion. He was greedy and cruel and threw prickle arrows at anyone who disagreed with him.

The animals all got together to discuss what they should do. They had to get rid of the hedgehog king. They talked and talked but none of them knew what to do. Then they heard a little voice on the ground, 'Can I say something?' The animals looked down and saw a worm. They began to laugh, 'You! You're too tiny! What can you do?' They didn't take the worm seriously. But the worm was strong. 'I know what to do.' So the animals all agreed to let the worm try.

First the worm went to see the lion and asked him to promise to be a better king, to be kind and fair to all the animals. The lion promised. Then the worm sent a message to the hedgehog that there was a better king than him and he should meet him at the pine tree for a battle, to see who was the strongest.

The hedgehog went to the pine tree and waited. He waited and waited, but he couldn't see anyone. Then he felt something under the earth, something was tickling his belly. He rolled himself into a round ball and he rolled this way and that way. But the tickling continued. The hedgehog started to laugh. He laughed and he laughed and he laughed, and he couldn't stop. He laughed uncontrollably. 'Stop!' he managed to say, 'Stop, please stop! I can't stand it.' 'I'll only stop if you promise to go away and never come back,' said the worm. 'OK,' said the hedgehog. That was the last they saw of him.

The worm went back to the lion and told him he could be king again, but that he must keep his promise and be a good king. The lion felt humble, 'Maybe I am strong, but you, though you are tiny, you have done something that I couldn't do. I will use my power for good from now on.' And that's what the lion did.

Cath: Thank you. I really like hearing you tell that story!

Ramy: My uncle would often stop in the middle of a story and ask us a question. When he told us the hedgehog story he stopped and asked us what we thought the worm would do. I remember my brother said that the worm had a gun! That made us laugh. But the story helped us see another point of view. It helped us to ask questions and to be curious.

The Travelling Storyteller

FROM SAM ALLO'S BLOG
(EDITED BY CHRISTINE WILLISON)

It was time to make marmalade. I had just returned from my travels to Australia in 2015, where I had been visiting my two older daughters and my four grandchildren, whilst also taking the opportunity to tell stories at Collingwood College, the Steiner school in Melbourne attended by my grandchildren, also at Footscray Library nearby. After unpacking my bags and dealing with three months' worth of laundry, it was finally marmalade time. Having received my annual delivery of 6 kilos of organic

Seville oranges, pre-ordered before I made my trip, I set to preparing the ingredients. And then the phone rang. It was my local library, apologising for disturbing me in my jetlag. (The joy of living in Wales is that everyone knows where you live, when you've been away, how long you've been away and when you've returned.) 'There is a storyteller here from Brittany and he is asking if there is a storyteller living locally, he needs some food, probably a shower and a bed for the night, and we thought of you,' explained the librarian.

I agreed to come straight away. It was there that I first met Sam Allo, from Brittany. I brought him home, shared a lunch of home-made soup with him and was delighted to hear about his travels through Wales and many places across the globe.

Sam is following the ancient tradition of the itinerant storyteller, he travels around the world with a small bag on his back and very little money. He relies on stories to provide him with his food and a bed for the night. He was delighted to find that his Breton was easily understood by children in Welsh-medium schools, with many words and numbers in common. He also tells in English.

After lunch he set to helping with the marmalade-making. He was adept chopping oranges, then he offered to wash-up whilst the conserve was bubbling in the maslin pan. At the bottling stage he gave me a tip which I still employ: store the jars of hot preserve upside-down to ensure a perfect sealing lid.

In the evening after supper, we sat by the fire and exchanged stories beyond midnight.

What a delightful man and how excited I was to discover a real troubadour, travelling with (maybe) a change of clothes and a toothbrush and little else, relying on his wits, his stories, music and dance to enable his travel.

The following material is taken, with Sam's permission, from his blog, samuelallo.com.

I leave you my blog of this new trip, if you want, feel free to mention anything you want about travelling and trading the oral tradition as a way of life. The aim of my trips is to share culture with the people different from me. I travel by foot and hitch-hiking. I never use money for travelling so no bus or taxi, but occasional air travel to cross the ocean. I trust the people that I meet on the way, most of them will help me. I never use hotels, hostels or paid-for accommodation, I have no tent. I always manage to find a place. I travel like a troubadour, I share the culture from my land (Bretagne in the west of France). I offer songs, dances, storytelling, juggling and music in the place I go. I stop in many schools, houses, orphanages, retired people houses, jails, I have slept in houses, farms, schools and other places ... When I meet a group, I ask them to share something with me. I have collected and shared many stories, poems, dances and much music.

I don't say that what I write is truth, they are just the ideas of a person who walks in different countries.

In my trips, I try to show that it is possible to live and share. The people of all the world can help each other, can share if they can be trusted by the others ... If you have something to offer (which is not money), you can share (games, songs, dances, stories, discussion, cooking, help ...).

In my first trip, in 2003, I went from France to China and crossed thirty-five countries in thirteen months (east of Europe, Russia, Iran, Pakistan, China) then I crossed the United States and Canada. During that trip, I went to 100 schools.

Three years later, in 2006, I did a second trip from Canada to Argentina without spending money (just sharing stories), then I took a plane from Chile to New Zealand, got a boat lift to Australia. After travelling across Australia, I took a plane to South Africa and hitch-hiked back to France through East Africa, Middle East and east of Europe, it took me twenty-one months to cross those forty-eight countries. I only slept fifteen times outside and more than 600 times in houses, schools and shops. I went to schools in 300 places where I met kids, prisoners and old people.

The idea of the trip is walking and sharing. It is very successful and rewarding you just need to trust and to be willing to learn about the difference. Open your heart to the meetings.

This is an experience that my heart tells me to live. I just want to share it with you. I won't keep doing that forever. But once I stop, I will try to carry on sharing the message of peace and sharing with a great respect of Mother Earth.

Thanks for the help on the road.

I hope to meet you again.

'Don't dream of your life but live your dreams...'

Touched by the moments shared with the migrants in Calais, I decided to go and see some of them in England and, aware of the chance to cross the borders with my French passport, I will make the opposite trip to join the refugee camps in Greece. I did not give myself time limit for this trip, my goal is to share stories, songs, dances, discussions with the people I will meet on my way. I travel without a tent and without a phone. I am able to celebrate these chance encounters and have opportunities to meet people every night.

I found Emad the Syrian in Stockton near Newcastle, Abdul the Sudanese in Manchester, Ammar (Emad's brother) in Cardiff, Mohammed the Bedouin in Glasgow. The stories of each one is very touching and very hard. Everyone would like to see their families and friends back home, but for security reasons they had to leave. They now know they have to rebuild a life in their new country. I understand and sympathise with the difficulty of rebuilding after having lost everything (materially but also culturally – language, family ties, friendship, culture, country).

I learned a song in Arabic from a veiled woman in the Newcastle Public Library. She was originally from Saudi Arabia and was very happy to teach me a lullaby in her mother tongue.

I then learned an Albanian song from a refugee, the song talks about Albanian attachment to their country.

You can read Sam's heart-rending and joyous stories, poems and songs from many places on his blog. I have included some examples below.

From Syria

I will continue to hope even if some have lost hope. Continue to love even if others distil hatred. Continue to build even if others destroy. Continue talking about peace even in the fog of war. Continue to illuminate even in deep darkness. Continue to sow even if others are harassing crops. Continue to scream even if others remain silent. And I will draw smiles on faces in tears. I will bring help when I see suffering. I will offer reasons of joy, where there is only suffering. I will invite to walk again the one who has stopped in the way. And I would hold my arms towards those who feel exhausted.

Syria, I miss you 04/06/2015

I started my journey into the unknown future. In a dangerous inflatable boat, I had 36 days of travelling on foot through Europe chased by police, I passed through eleven countries to reach my dream, the safety and my new life. When I reached Dover (England), I cried, I kissed the ground and thanked my God, I am finally here.

I came without any English, without friends, without my family. Because of that, I started to help other asylum seekers and refugees and also English people who need help, whatever was their religion or colour, because now I know what it means to be alone in another country with different language and different culture.

10/07/2015 Fate and destiny

Sometimes in your life things happen, you can't expect or imagine that will do. I had everything in my life in Syria, more than any single young man can dream to have.

Suddenly, I lost everything, this is the first time in my life I am far away from my family, I lost my home, many of my friends have died, I lost my

love, my university, my car, my livelihood, my home town and my home country. My parents said it is ok, we are not sad; the most important thing for us is you and your brothers, you are far away from us, but at least we know you are safe.

Last few years I had been in a very bad situation; many things had happened made me feel like it is the end of my life. I had suffered too much, that was enough to make me decide to make a decision: kill myself or get up from under the rubble and debris.

Sam reports

The number of people living in the jungle (the refugee camp in Calais) has doubled since June. Approximately 9,000 people now live in this place in conditions of hunger and poverty. A human being who flees from war should be able to maintain his dignity. I still find it aberrant [*sic*] that France and England who continue to sell weapons are simply trying to 'manage' the migratory crisis with fences. Will these weapons be used to make peace? Just listening to the stories of people who left their homes and families to escape danger, to abandon their families, friends, love, language, culture and careers then to embark on a journey without return. After their experiences, they are ready to risk their lives to reach this place of peace.

Sam continues his journey
4 September 2016: Switzerland

The Swiss seem very surprised when I explain that my travel arrangement works perfectly, and that people are very hospitable. Farmers agreed that I could sleep in their barn or I was invited into homes. I have managed to work without money, only with barter – stories, music and pictures.

I went to meet the speakers of the fourth official language of Switzerland (Romansh). I am touched by the way the last 25,000 speakers take care of their heritage. I can't help comparing the situation of Switzerland with its four official languages, which means that most people are trilingual or quadrilingual here, and the situation in France where regional languages are not recognised and valued. Yet it is these regions and their diversities that make up the cultural wealth of a country and its tolerance towards other cultures.

The Romansh have impressed me with the warmth of their welcome and their curiosity with regard to other minority languages.

Here is one of their poems that I translated with a teacher (imagine the scene in a village at 1,600m altitude in the Alps a century ago):

The silent village dreams listening to the creek singing the old tales
From time to time, the watchman makes his song heard, and once he has
    passed, silence resumes its place
The hours which the bell-tower strikes close, tremble in the air and break
    in the wind
At the top in the sky, the golden stars, eternal spenders, shine
Why are you beating so hard, oh my heart?

12 September 2016: Passage through Austria

A wonderful moment of sharing with a class that seems like a refuge for Syrian, Aramaic, Afghan, Turkish and Chechen children who create new friendly ties with Austrian children. For the first time, I venture to tell in German. I tell a story of Breton Yann and his cow, children help me and take pleasure in helping an adult to express themselves in a language that they quickly have to master to be able to do their schooling. The dances of Breton women and those brought back from trips are appreciated. The children are too shy or a little intimidated to share a song in their language. Not easy to 'melt' into a new culture while not losing the richness of its roots. Teachers hope that these children will not be displaced again because the difficulties of the journey they underwent brought them to life enormous instability. If adults allow it, they will finally be able to cultivate some new roots.

23 September 2016: Hungary

Reunion with old friends. What a joy to find families met during previous trips.

The children have grown, the sharing is fruitful, and the heat of the reunion gives me a lot of strength to continue this journey.

I also meet Abdul Aziz, he just got his right to asylum in Hungary but is afraid of the attitude of people. The latter show their hostility towards the refugees.

When I went to Hungary a few days before the referendum, I witnessed the campaign of fear in the media.

However, Hungarians take me in, offer me accommodation for one night, a meal … Finally, the vote is 98 per cent against the reception of refugees. Even the Hungarians who went to work a few years in England and returned home vote against the reception of migrants: with a media campaign of terror, this does not surprise anyone.

4 October 2016: Bosnia

I go to a school and find that the children of the Christian, Muslim and Orthodox communities are now separated. They learn a different story. They do not go to the same schools. They speak the same language but do not co-exist. Adults are sad to see that their children will not be able to live multiculturalism. Political will is to separate people. As a traveller, I am welcomed into communities that do not know each other.

7 October 2016: Montenegro

A country has very varied and beautiful nature. I cross the mountain. One evening I knocked on the door of a small farm. The elderly woman is timid, she calls her children, then the doctor. It is the latter who speaks English who will give the approval for me to lodge in the barn.

9 October 2016: Kosovo

I had a surprising reception. Probably the warmest of all this trip and yet the information about this country had not been very positive. The vehicles stop to help me even before I stretched my thumb. Communication is relatively easy because younger people know how to speak English, French or German.

A class from a school in Calais agrees to correspond with this school to share cultures and ideas, to fight against prejudices towards the inhabitants of countries whose nationals have fled.

11 October 2016: Macedonia

In this country I feel the population divided. The Macedonians and Albanians of Macedonia speak two languages and no effort to bring them closer seems envisaged.

Everyone welcomes me very well and complains of the others. I spend one night in a mosque. I am told, 'This place is the house of God. Allah is the same God as that of other human beings, so you can rest here.'

In a school, the children show me the dance Makedonsko.

14 October 2016: Greece

On my first night in Greece, it was cold outside, I managed to be accepted by a farmer and it is symbolic to be warmed by the heat of the potatoes in the hangar where he allows me to sleep.

I am shown a video of Crete which testifies to the exasperation of men towards the politicians.

I spent ten days in the city of Thessaloniki offering juggling and storytelling activities for Syrian, Kurdish and Afghan children in the refugee camps. In this city, I met very hospitable people. Everyone in his own way helps refugees who are looking for a solution to live peacefully.

Traders offer food that must be eaten the same day (sandwiches, bread, fruits, vegetables), volunteers distribute it. People have been opening safe houses for years to allow people fleeing the war to rest at night. An association 'Antigoni' offers activities for children in the camps. It is with Antigoni that I am associated to propose activities of storytelling.

I have illustrated the stories to be able to tell them – in spite of the language barrier – to children, Syrians (Arabic language), Kurds (Kurdish language), Afghans (Dari or Pashto according to their origin).

This journey allows me to hear human testimonies confirming that our so-called 'truths' are only illusions. The more I advance the less certainties I have. I try to inform myself of the local population but when I do not know anyone I am in the same situation as the others: should I believe what the media are saying controlled by the financial powers or the states? What source of information can I trust?

30 October 2016: Island of Lesbos

Here the refugees find themselves trapped, obliged to seek asylum in Greece or turn back. Yet some want to join their families in another European state. Some people ask me for advice: You who have travelled, who has seen many peoples, who has received the wisdom of the road – if you were in my place, what would you do?

Who can give advice to people fleeing the violence of a state and find themselves faced with the violence of a European institution?

Ideas, thoughts, compassion, yes, I can share, but that's all.

After twenty days on the island of Lesbos, marvellous sharing of stories naturally thanks to the drawings that illustrate the stories, I decide to continue my journey as storyteller. I have heard so many injustices in recent months between Calais and Lesvos. I will now continue to carry the word of those who cannot cross borders, carry stories of hope to those who will want to share a moment with me. I carry in my heart all these people met, all these friends that I leave behind me with the hope that our paths will re-cross.

Itaca (Ithaca)

When you go on a trip to Ithaca
pray for the path to be long,
full of adventures, full of discoveries.
Pray for the journey to be long,
and many mornings where your eyes will discover
an ignored port,

and many cities where you will seek knowledge.
Keep the idea of Ithaca always at heart.
You must reach it, it is your destiny,
but does not force the crossing.
It is better that it lasts a long time
and be thou old when thou shalt anchor,
rich of all that you will have amassed on the way
without expecting any more riches.

Ithaca gave you the beautiful journey,
without her, you would not have gone.
And if you find it poor, it is not that you
be deceived.
The wisdom you have gained allows you
to understand the meaning of the Ithaca.

II

Further, you need to go further
the trees that imprison you
and when you have overtaken them
try not to stop.
Further, go further and further
than the present that still enchains you
and when you are delivered resume
the road again.
Further, always, much further, further
that the following day,
and when you think you have arrived,
know how to find new ways.

III

Bon voyage to the warriors
who are faithful to their people.
That the god of the winds be favourable
to the sail of their ship.
Despite their old struggle they find
the pleasure of bodies
the most loving.
Fill the coveted nets of stars
full of felicities,
full of knowledge.

Bon voyage to the warriors if they are loyal
to their people.
Despite their old struggle that love fills
their generous body they find the paths
old desires full of happiness,
full of knowledge.

23 November 2016: Georgia: tradition of hospitality

New country; a new alphabet. I love this feeling of having to find other ways to communicate than with the word.

An evening with professional footballers super friendly (who earn 250 euros per month), a decent salary here.

29 November 2016: Generous Armenia

I am told that a road was built thanks to the money of the Armenian refugees who live in Europe and the United States. I am very moved to see that after several generations, Armenians continue to cherish the country from their roots.

At school, I am compared to the troubadour Armenian-Georgian and Azeri 'Sayad Nova', what an honour!

What touches me is the welcome in the families: Here, one or three generations live under the same roof.

5 December 2016: Georgia the return

I come back to share stories in schools and make my request for a Russian Visa.

The drawings (in Greece) offered to me by young Iranians, Pakistanis, Somalis, Afghans, Syrians allow me to tell stories in schools.

After waiting for the Russian Visa, I can continue my journey.

12 December: Russia: A wonderful welcome

I discover the cultures of the republics of southern Russia: Ingouches Tchetchenes.

I regretfully leave Russia after receiving a fabulous welcome. My month's visa ends.

I always appreciate my encounter with winter, the steps and hitchhiking.

After about a year on the road, I sometime get mentally or physically tired but the meetings and the sharings help me to carry on and find energy ... Some days, I tell stories in a home, others in a hotel and others in the street, meeting all those people walking on the same earth, all responsible of taking good care of her.

If you come across Sam, please offer him a bed and a meal – you will get more than you bargained for.

The Storytellers

Christine Willison

www.christinestories.co.uk

Christine Willison has been telling stories since the 1980s. Her repertoire is drawn from Ireland, where her paternal grandmother hailed from, from Eastern Europe, where some of her maternal ancestors originated and from Wales, where she has lived since the late 1990s. She lives in an ancient long house, which has been the backdrop for many stories and which has inspired her book *The Long House,* which tells the (fictional) story of the house from ancient times. She has published *Pembrokeshire Folk Tales* with The History Press.

John Row

www.johnrow.com

John Row, veteran of the British festival scene, is a storyteller, poet and painter who has peddled his wares on four continents. Performing since the late 1960s, he has appeared anywhere that would pay him and many places that didn't.

His chapbooks of poetry include *Stewed Tea and Breadcrumbs*, *Where There's Muck*, *Arrested Development*, *Declaration of Independence* and *Impure Theatre*. His book of poetry for children, *The Pong Machine*, has sold several thousand copies, as has his book of traditional tales from around the world, *Out of the Hat*.

He is currently collecting local tales from Transylvania, where he has a house.

Kevin Crossley-Holland

www.kevincrossley-holland.com

Kevin is a patron of the Society for Storytelling and the Story Museum. Following his new version for younger readers of the *Norse Myths* (2017), Walker Books will publish an illustrated edition of his *British Folk Tales* in 2018, and he is now working with Chris Riddell on a one-volume *Arthur* (2019). Well-known poet, translator from Anglo-Saxon and prize-winning children's author (the *Arthur* trilogy, *Gatty's Tale*) he has been awarded honorary doctorates by Anglia Ruskin and Worcester Universities, and is an Honorary Fellow at St Edmund Hall, Oxford, and Fellow of the Royal Society of Literature.

Jack Zipes

https://en.wikipedia.org/wiki/Jack_Zipes

Jack Zipes is Professor Emeritus of German and Comparative Literature at the University of Minnesota. In addition to his scholarly work, he is an active storyteller in public schools and has worked with children's theatres in Europe and the United States. Some of his recent publications include: *Why Fairy Tales Stick: The Evolution and Relevance of a Genre* (2006), *The Irresistible Fairy Tale: The Cultural and Social History of a Genre* (2012), *The Golden Age of Folk and Fairy Tales: From the Brothers Grimm to Andrew Lang* (2013), *Grimm Legacies: The Magic Power of Fairy Tales* (2014). Most recently he has published *The Sorcerer's Apprentice: An Anthology of Magical Tales* (2017*)* and *Tales of Wonder: Retelling Fairy Tales through Picture Postcards* (2017).

Jack is a patron of the Society for Storytelling.

Taffy Thomas MBE

First Laureate for Storytelling

www.taffythomas.co.uk

Taffy Thomas has been living in Grasmere for well over thirty years. He was the founder of legendary 1970s folk theatre company Magic Lantern, who used shadow puppets and storytelling to illustrate folk tales. After surviving a major stroke in 1985 he used oral storytelling as speech therapy, which led him to find a new career working as a storyteller.

He set up the Storytellers Garden and the Northern Centre for Storytelling at Church Stile in Grasmere, Cumbria.

He was asked to become patron of the Society for Storytelling and was awarded an MBE for Services to Storytelling and Charity in the Millennium Honours list in 2001.

In January 2010 he was appointed as the first UK Storyteller Laureate at The British Library. He was awarded the Gold Badge, highest honour of the English Folk Dance and Song Society, that same year.

At the 2013 British Awards for Storytelling Excellence (BASE) Taffy received the award for outstanding male storyteller and also received the award for outstanding storytelling performance for his piece 'Ancestral Voices'.

More recently he has become patron of Open Storytellers, a charity that works to enrich and empower the lives of people marginalised because of learning and communication difficulties, and also the patron of the East Anglian Storytelling Festival.

Hugh Lupton

www.hughlupton.com

Hugh Lupton's interest in traditional music, in street theatre, in live poetry, and in myth, resulted in him becoming a professional storyteller in 1981.

For twelve years he toured Britain with the Company of Storytellers (with Ben Haggarty and Sally Pomme Clayton). Their work was instrumental in stimulating a nationwide revival of interest in storytelling.

AN INTRODUCTION TO STORYTELLING

Since the mid-1990s he has worked as a solo performer and collaborator. In 2006 he and Daniel Morden were awarded the Classical Association Prize for 'the most significant contribution to the public understanding of the classics'.

His work with musician Chris Wood has resulted in commissions from Radio 3 and the 'Song of the Year' at the BBC Radio 2 Folk Awards.

He tells stories from many cultures, but his particular passion is for the hidden layers of the British landscape and the stories and ballads that give voice to them.

He has published many collections of folk tales and myths, including *Norfolk Folk Tales* for The History Press. His first novel, *The Ballad of John Clare*, was published in 2010 and he has recently finished a second, *The Assembly of the Severed Head* (2018).

Michael Harvey

www.michaelharvey.org

Michael has told stories both as a solo performer and with other artists throughout the UK and Europe as well as festivals in North and South America. Most of his work is in either English or Welsh and occasionally both at the same time! He is a familiar performer in the UK festival and club scene and draws particular inspiration from the Welsh oral heritage and landscape. He combines depth of material with lightness of delivery which is timed and paced to perfection and minted fresh for every audience.

He works in collaboration with the production company Adverse Camber touring 'Hunting the Giant's Daughter' and 'Dreaming the Night Field', faithful and contemporary retellings of Welsh mythology. In 2011 he was awarded a Major Creative Wales Award, took part in the 3rd Labo at La Maison du Conte in Paris, and was a featured teller at the 2012 National Storytelling Festival in Jonesborough, Tennessee.

Anne E. Stewart

www.anneestewart.com.au

Storyteller, writer, broadcaster, MC and public speaker. When you've been telling stories as long as I have (starting in 1977) a diversity of jobs and storytelling experiences come your way. I have told stories in some of Australia's major cultural institutions, art galleries, schools and libraries, as well as on ABC radio and TV. I have been an invited guest at storytelling festivals throughout Australia, the UK and in Mexico, Colombia and Iran. I've developed skills to be a consummate MC with the ability to create shows tailored to audience needs. I run storytelling workshops and masterclasses, and lately have started to develop my digital storytelling skills.

Please browse my website to learn more about the art of storytelling, or stay a while and listen to a story or two. I focus on the shared stories of Australia, honouring Indigenous, Celtic, Asian and World stories.

Tony Cooper

www.tonytaleweaver.com

Tony Cooper is an accidental storyteller thrown into the art by an unexpectedly long life. The onset of multiple sclerosis in his thirties drove him out of a failing career in further education into telling big, fancy lies for profit. He is still getting away with it after thirty years at the job.

Chip Colquhoun

www.snailtales.org

Chip Colquhoun began performing professionally in 2007. He's since toured seven countries, represented the Oxford Reading Tree online, and written the EU guide to storytelling for schools, as well as three collections of folk tales, including *Cambridgeshire Folk Tales for Children* and *Who Made England? The Saxon–Viking Race to Create a Country* (both published by The History Press).

Pete Castle

www.petecastle.co.uk

www.factsandfiction.co.uk

Pete Castle was born a 'Man of Kent' in 1947 but has lived most of his adult life in the East Midlands. Now he considers Derbyshire his home and has a large selection of local songs and stories in his repertoire. He met and married Sue while they were both at Bretton Hall College of Education and they live in Belper. In the past Pete has worked all over the UK and, occasionally, abroad. He continues to work although most of it is now more local.

Pete has recorded prolifically, both song and storytelling, and is author of three books for The History Press: *Derbyshire Folk Tales*, *Nottinghamshire Folk Tales*, and *Where Dragons Soar: Animal Folk Tales of the British Isles*.

Michael Wilson

M.Wilson2@lboro.ac.uk

Michael Wilson is Professor of Drama at Loughborough University, where he runs a number of research projects on various aspects of storytelling. He is also Visiting Professor of Applied Storytelling at the University of South Wales, where he was a co-founding Director of The George Ewart Evans Centre for Storytelling. He has published widely on storytelling and is author of *Storytelling and Theatre* (Palgrave MacMillan).

Deb Winter

www.deborahwinter.co.uk

Deb Winter has delighted audiences across Wales and the South West with a winning mixture of high energy, irrepressible humour and something wavering between originality and eccentricity.

Having won the coveted 'Yarn-spinner of the Year' award at Bristol Storyfest in 2015, Deb was invited to bring three new shows (Behind the Veil, Red Shoes, Trysts & Promises) to the festival.

In 2015, 2016 and 2017, working with musicians Ailsa Mair Hughes and Fiona Barrow. Despite being a relative newcomer, Deb has quickly become a popular teller on the story club circuit and been booked by a diverse range of venues and festivals such as: Cheltenham Science Festival, Tenby Arts Festival, Priddy & EOTR festivals, Swansea Fringe, WOMAD, National Trust, Pembrokeshire Coast, Fforest, West Wales Arts Centre, Transition Bro Gwaun.

She has co-hosted Tenby Storytelling Café with Phil Okwedy, and went on to set up Fishguard Storytelling/Straeon Gwaun. She was awarded one of six commissions across Wales for the 2016 Gwanwyn Festival, funded by Arts Council Wales/Age Cymru, to develop a collaborative piece inspired by Celtic mythology.

A trainer and facilitator by background, and a prize-winning short story writer, Deb also leads popular Storytelling Skills, Improv and Creative Writing workshops as well as working in the Storytelling for Health field.

Dr Emily Underwood-Lee

http://storytelling.research.southwales.ac.uk

Emily is Research Fellow at the George Ewart Evans Centre for Storytelling at the University of South Wales. Her research focuses on women's performance, autobiographical stories and the body in a variety of contexts, including feminist performance art, narratives of illness and performance, and the maternal.

Eirwen Malin

eirwenmalin.wordpress.com

Eirwen worked in Wales in the third sector in the fields of adult education and the arts for nearly thirty years. Throughout that time she used storytelling to entertain, inform and influence. She has taken stories from Wales to Australia, New Zealand, Canada and the USA.

Eirwen has been a long-term, behind the scenes supporter of Beyond the Border Wales' International Storytelling Festival and since 2011, when it became an independent charity, been the Chair of the Board of Trustees.

In the past she worked as a freelance independent evaluator of arts in health projects and now finds herself instigator, artist and subject of her own arts in health project. 'Sorting the Sock Drawer' toured in Wales and the US during 2016–17 and is available for performance.

Liz Berg

lizbergstoryteller@gmail.com

Liz Berg lives in Cornwall where she writes in English, sings in Yiddish and English, and tells stories from Cornwall and her Jewish heritage with a Welsh accent.

Jackie Kerin

www.jackiekerin.com.au, storytellingvic.org.au

Jackie Kerin has a performance and writing background. She is a highly decorated storyteller working in the oral tradition and having won awards at two of the largest folk festivals in Australia: Port Fairy Folk Festival and Woodford. Her children's books *Lyrebird! A True Story* and *Phar Lap the Wonder Horse* are recognised by the Children's Book Council of Australia as being of excellence. Jackie is an active member of Storytelling Australia Victoria and supports events that share, promote and grow the oral tradition in all its forms.

Klara Miller-Fuhren

www.erzaehlkultur.net

At the age of 24 Klara graduated from Drama School in Paris and became an actress. Then she became a stage actress in Paris as well as touring France for ten years. Following that she lived a more spiritually-centered life in Vomperberg, Austria. When she started a family at the age of 40 she realised the uplifting influence of stories on her two children, which started her career as a storyteller, eventually mainly for adults.

Back in Bavaria now, she has regular storytelling dates in rehabilitation clinics all around the area, under the heading of 'Happy End Stories'. She also performs with pianists, harpists, and singer-songwriters from all over the world.

In the largest theatre between Munich and Salzburg she has a yearly production of spoken biographies of 'Fanny and Felix Mendelsson-Bartholdy', 'Debussy, Satie, Ravel', 'Ira and George Gershwin' and other famous composers with an internationally known pianist.

She is also a founder member of the German Storyteller Association (VEE).

Gary and Linda Kuntz

https://rapsstories.org/img_1263/

Gary and Linda Kuntz live in Gladstone, Missouri (the home of Happy Rock Park), a suburb of Kansas City, MO which is the western part of the Midwest. In their day jobs, Linda works at a public high school (9th–12th grade) teaching students with special needs who have cognitive and/or behavioural disorders. Gary is a computer programmer analyst and works in the airline reservation industry.

Linda has been telling stories all her life but no longer gets into trouble for spinning a tall tale. She has competed in Tall Tale and Liar's Contests, but her favourite stories contain a universal truth. Linda enjoys telling tales from around the world to audiences of all ages.

Gary tells a mixture of stories: folk, classic, personal, humour, drama, and tall tales. All of his stories are 100 per cent, completely, absolutely, true – at least, while he tells them. He is the 2013 winner of the Kansas Storytelling Festival Tall Tales Contest and his name is inscribed on the handle of the Golden Shovel, along with the other winners of that contest.

Fiona Collins

fiona.storyteller@btinternet.com

Fiona Collins is a storyteller who tells traditional tales from around the world, with special interests in stories of strong women and girls, and the Tales of Wales.

A professional storyteller for over twenty-five years, Fiona works with all ages and abilities in a diverse range of settings. She lives in north-east Wales and tells stories in English, her mother tongue, and Welsh, her second language, working bilingually with Welsh learners.

Fiona has written four books of Welsh folk tales, all published by The History Press: *Denbighshire Folk Tales*, *Wrexham County Folk Tales*, *Ancient Legends Retold: The Legend of Pryderi*, and *North Wales Folk Tales for Children*.

Uncle Larry Walsh

http://footscrayarts.com/profile\uncle-larry-walsh

Uncle Larry Walsh is an Aboriginal elder based in Victoria. He was taken from his family as a young child. It was Australia's policy in the twentieth century to forcibly place Aboriginal children with white families. He is one of the 'Stolen' generation.

He has been a strong leader for young people making sense of the collision of two worlds – that of Aboriginal culture and later white settlement in metropolitan Melbourne. He brings to the attention of the world, the stolen lands, the stolen people and the attempted decimation of native culture.

He particularly loves working with the younger generation as he sees them as the torchbearers of the future. Inspired by his local Aboriginal

community, and his Kulin ancestral blood connections to his country, Uncle Larry is an Elder in Melbourne who focuses specifically on storytelling, ensuring the cultural continuity of his ancient oral traditions.

Cath Little

www.cathlittle.co.uk

Cardiff storyteller and singer Cath Little has 'rough magic' in her voice and in her words 'the gift of the story shines through'. She has a strong sense that stories have the power to connect us to one another, to the land and to the people who once lived here.

Cath has told stories at Beyond the Border Storytelling Festival, Glastonbury Festival of Performing Arts and the BBC Proms Folk Day. She regularly tells at the National Museum of Wales. Cath helps run the Cardiff Storytelling Circle and curates their seasonal concerts, Tales for the Turning Year. She keeps busy telling stories in local schools and runs a Family Storytelling Club for her community. She also runs a storytelling circle at Oasis, a Cardiff charity which offers a warm Welsh welcome to refugees and asylum seekers.

Cath draws inspiration from The Matter of Britain, the native tales of these islands, from her Irish and English heritage and from her Welsh homeland. The most exciting thing she has done so far is to be a part of Y Mabinogi – an unforgettable bilingual retelling of all four branches of the Mabinogion in one day at Aberystwyth Arts Centre, curated by Peter Stevenson. Cath is passionate about sharing these treasures, gifts from the ancestors, and in her belief that the stories belong to us all and are meant to be heard.

Sam Allo

http://samuelallo.com

I travel alone; people are more likely to talk to an individual and will be less intimidated. I find that discussions are richer, and people will reveal their aspirations, dreams, poetry and stories in a tête-à-tête rather than in a group. I make my own decisions and travel according to my intuition and my feelings. The project is very personal, and I don't want to impose it on anyone else. It has taken shape little by little.

I hitchhike without exhibiting valuable objects like glasses, wristwatch or branded clothing, so I don't look like a tourist. I walk with the people of the places I visit, I take in the atmosphere and the smell of the place.

Discussions are between equals, person to person. I try to break up the inequality ratios: I am convinced that everyone, regardless of age or orientation, can teach me something.

I employ many skills alongside storytelling such as juggling, playing the flute or guitar, singing, dancing, and playing games.

About the Cover Illustrator

Paul Jackson started his professional career as an artist in 1977, making ceramics in porcelain. By 1985 he was selling his unique sculptures all over the world. He started a design company in 1989, and then in 1993 went on his first course of storytelling at St Donats, with Pomme Clayton as his tutor. There followed a full-time career in storytelling, visiting over 2,000 schools and telling stories in theatres, churches, boats and even in a hollow tree. Paul is passionate about the importance of stories for all ages. He also uses them to inspire his own writing and for his ceramics and book illustrations. The cover illustration for this book is based on twelve of his favourite stories.

In 2015, Paul joined the Board of Trustees of the Society of Storytelling to help invigorate it. In 2017 he became the Chair of the society and together with a dedicated team of storytellers, including Christine Willison who compiled and edited this book, helped the Society to blossom and become relelvant and accessible again. This book is very much part of that positive change.

Society *for* Storytelling

Since 1993, The Society for Storytelling has championed the ancient art of oral storytelling and its long and honourable history – not just as entertainment, but also in education, health, and inspiring and changing lives. Storytellers, enthusiasts and academics support and are supported by this registered charity to ensure the art is nurtured and developed throughout the UK.

Many activities of the Society are available to all, such as locating storytellers on the Society website, taking part in our annual National Storytelling Week at the start of every February, purchasing our quarterly magazine Storylines, or attending our Annual Gathering – a chance to revel in engaging performances, inspiring workshops, and the company of like-minded people.

You can also become a member of the Society to support the work we do. In return, you receive free access to Storylines, discounted tickets to the Annual Gathering and other storytelling events, the opportunity to join our mentorship scheme for new storytellers, and more. Among our great deals for members is a 30% discount off titles from The History Press.

For more information, including how to join, please visit

www.sfs.org.uk